A Treasury of Special Wedding Ceremonies

Love Stories and the Power of Ritual

Crystal Yarlott

This book is dedicated to the couples in Ukraine who have taken a stand for the right to love in peace.

CONTENTS

Holiday Ceremonies

Addendum

"Rituals, anthropologists will tell us, are about transformation. The rituals we use for marriage ... are as elaborate as they are because we associate the ritual with a major life passage, the crossing of a critical threshold, or in other words, with transformation."
Abraham Verghese

INTRODUCTION

Telling a couple's love story is an art. For an officiant, this means finding the most meaningful, joyful, and reflective ways to acknowledge the importance of a couple's commitment to love. A special wedding ceremony is one of the brushstrokes an officiant uses to paint the picture of what a couple values in life. The colors they use may be the golds of their cultural background, the pinks of joy and humor, or the reds, blues and greens of those things they are passionate about.

Over the thirty plus years that I've led wedding ceremonies, my couples have told me stories of traditions that are part of their cultural heritage. They've brought me the special rituals they admired, and told me why others weren't important to them. The fact that they were going to walk down an aisle, stand together, and exchange vows and rings reveals there's a captivating power in ritual that gets engaged whether the couple is aware of it or not.

For example, walking down an aisle is a ritual. It's a passageway into an important new chapter of their life. Getting more dressed up than they will ever be again in their life, like countless couples before them have done, is also a ritual. Love is called through ritual to bear all things, believe all things, hope for and endure all things including extreme nervousness. Vowing to love each other publicly elevates these beliefs and are made more enduring through the power of ritual.

This *Treasury of Special Wedding Ceremonies* is an exploration of the unique traditions that cultures have relied on to affirm the power of love and commitment for decades, even centuries, and takes a new look or approach to the way these rituals have always been done. It's meant to be a resource book that makes it easier for an officiant to be creative. The Treasury helps elevate the art of how to best tell the story of two people's decision to make Love the guiding principle in their life.

Certain ceremonies have their historical background included, for example, Bread and Salt, Jumping the Broom, and Stefana Crowns. That way you know where the ceremony originated and what its inner meanings are. There are bold ceremonies like the Halloween Ceremony, Bourbon, and the Truce Bells. You'll find common ceremonies you may have done many times yourself, but always with an extra option called "A Bit of Dazzle." The Dazzle introduces you to how you can add a few more layers to the entire ceremony's meaning.

The pre-written scripts are a place for you to begin from and needless to say, are not set in stone. But there are set-up suggestions, and links to vendors who have the elements that are needed to complete the special ceremony. Providing the essential elements is usually the couple's responsibility but sharing the links to get necessary supplies makes their process easier which is always a plus.

I am not insinuating that every couple wants a ceremony that includes a cultural or creative element. They don't. But I believe all couples want to feel their love is special and worth the effort their officiant makes to represent how important the love they've found is.

During the first waves of the Covid-19 pandemic, weddings downsized considerably. Where couples had depended on a big party to round out their special day, a ceremony with their closest family and friends in attendance became most important. Special ceremonies were key to making the event a remedy for their disappointment.

One couple who requested a "short and sweet" ceremony appreciated my suggestion that I include a simple special ceremony. "Your commitment to each other is a big deal. Without being preachy, I'd like to add a little something distinctive for you." She agreed, and seemed grateful an effort was being made to personalize their ceremony.

On the day of their wedding, we met at a public park situated on the beach. The bride dressed in a sexy, off-shoulder, white dress. The groom wore sunglasses, even in the shade, khaki shorts, and a white shirt which was starched and pressed. But neither the simplicity of the ceremony nor their casual approach to formality detracted from their dedication. The special ceremony they experienced was the Wedding Zen which is one of the ceremonies in this book. They. Loved. It.

Afterward, the bride's twenty-year old daughter took me aside, and whispered in my ear, "Thank you for making this special for my mother. It was so much nicer than the quickie ceremony that I settled for at the courthouse." The bride sent me a number of follow-up texts thanking me for more than the signing ceremony she'd originally requested. She mentioned that she was happy that it wasn't over in two minutes like it otherwise would have been.

Occasionally my couples, often my best researchers, send a script they'd like me to use. This is where the Handfasting Ceremony, the Arras and Lasso, Candle Lighting, Wedding Blanket and the Wedding Vase ceremonies have come from. I reworked words and added symbolism so that once the couple approves the script, their ceremony can be even more artful and meaningful.

There are couples who wanted some part of the ceremony to be completely different and more contemporary. Their openness inspired a completely new ritual which is where Stringing the Pearls, the Archway, a Marriage Between Equals, and Wall of Lights came from. Two other original ceremonies, Divorce and Wedding Zen came from other artistic officiants.

When a celebrant uses this resource of Special Wedding Ceremonies to help tell their couple's love story, they have taken their place as an artist. Based on the results a couple receives and then passes on for others to read in their reviews makes an officiant all the more desirable. Hire-able. Transformational. Sought after. Like a painting that appreciates over time, great reviews build up over time, and draw more and more wonderful couples to you. As officiants, we get to show our couples that we believe in the love they have found.

You are an artist and with love in your heart, you'll always be perfecting your art. The power of ritual will help your couples enjoy the colors and textures you bring to them, and make their ceremony truly memorable.

Crystal Yarlott
March, 2022

PREFACE

Weddings offer us a chance to be positive, happy, loving, caring, sharing, generous, thoughtful people. The act of attending a wedding is an opportunity to experience these traits, and this opportunity is itself a special ceremony.

Every little thing involved with attending a wedding or participating in a wedding is a special mini-event, from receiving announcements and save-the-dates, to marking a wedding on our calendar, to making travel plans and hotel arrangements, to deciding what to wear, what to gift and how quickly to RSVP. The wedding day is a series of rituals and ceremonies, from a welcome gift bag at the hotel to a welcoming arrival at a venue to the thrills of reunion, the wedding ceremony, signature drinks at cocktail hour, the dinner, the speeches, the thanking, the tears, the dancing…even the electric slide is a kind of inclusive ritual. Boogie oogie oogie.

Special ceremonies within a wedding ceremony ask something of us that most of us are hard-wired against: slowing down. They are optional, additional, and metaphorical. Some of them involve props, or other people, or rehearsing. They entail research and understanding.

But they are worth it. Two people dedicating their lives to each other, offering to give of themselves to another person for the rest of their lives – that's a big deal and it's important for everyone to understand that it's a big deal. It's worth slowing down to bless rings, share wine, paint a painting, send a pair of keys to the heavens on the strings of balloons, light a candle, jump over a broom, don a mala, don a crown of flowers, don a lei, circle the ceremonial space in a meaningful blanket, to be hoisted onto the shoulders of strong uncles, to assemble a puzzle or take a moment to take in the moment.

Everyone at the wedding has the rest of their lives to do whatever they do at whatever speed they please. Weddings offer us the chance to slow down, to mark a very special event by taking steps to understand the importance of the event as deeply as one can understand anything.

Any officiant worth his or her salt has a vast playbook of special ceremonies (or rituals, or rites, whatever you'd like to call them) that can help a couple slow down on their special day, to mark and honor the miracle of interpersonal human chemistry.

In this treasury, my colleague Crystal Yarlott, has assembled a marvelous toolkit for couples and officiants, myself included. She clearly presents each ceremony and provides sample dialogue, instructions and alternatives. Her 'bits of dazzle' are invitations to creativity.

It's an honor for me to have one of my own rituals included in this collection (Wedding Zen), which I created as a way for couples to breathe during one of the most magical moments of their lives, in between the super-charged ceremonial buildup and its chaotic release into party-time. In all honesty, I was inspired by such diverse influences as Jon Stewart's 'Moment of Zen' from The Daily Show and from CBS Sunday Morning's 'Moment in Nature'. Both always pleased me with their simplicity, their invitation to notice only what is. In a day and age where everything is recorded on video and in photos, I maintain that nothing can capture or preserve a moment like the human memory.

As T.S. Eliot wrote, 'There will be time, there will be time.' Each special ceremony included in this collection is an invitation to take time for something important. Special ceremonies deserve time, and every one of the ceremonies collected herein is worth the time. Enjoy!

Christopher Shelley, January 2022
Certified Life-Cycle Celebrant™ and Wedding Officiant
Author of Best. Ceremony. Ever.
(The countryman Press/W.W. Norton)
www.IlluminatingCeremonies.com

1 ACKNOWLEDGEMENT OF THOSE NOT PRESENT

What more could we offer to our couple than only a simple mentioning of the name of someone who influenced their life? The issue is to not make it so serious that citing their loved one makes them sad. That may be unavoidable but here are suggestions we can use to soften a couple's sadness.

1.   Make sure the couple is not trying to appease someone by mentioning someone's name who didn't really have an effect on their lives. Encourage your couple to only include those who meant something to them in a big way.

2.   If there are a lot of people to be mentioned, suggest they point them out in a program or set up a Table of Remembrances with their photos and mementos for guests to view. You don't want to be rattling off a lot of names so that it seems like a roll call.

3.   Ask them a question or two about how the person they want mentioned affected their life or what the deceased liked or would have liked (they may not have met their mate) about the person Partner1/Partner2 is marrying. Then weave this into the ceremony so it gives the words you've chosen to mention about the loved one more meaning and heart.

Option 1

I'd like to take this moment to mention that there are those who are close to [Couples Names] who could not travel to be with us here today, but whose thoughts and blessings are with them; and there are loved ones who are no longer here physically, but who are here in Spirit. Let's remember them now in a moment of silence.

Option 2

[Couples Names] wish to acknowledge those who were not able to travel here today but are with us in their hearts. Special thoughts and love are with (Names of the ones not present and their relationship to the couple) who are not here physically but shall always be present in the memories we have of them (Officiant can give an example of a special time or event they shared).

Option 3

On days like today that are special to us, we'd love to have everyone who ever meant something dear to us to be with us. But that is rarely the case, and today is no exception. But we know we are never separated in Spirit, because in Spirit there is no distance or time. Our couple would like to take a moment of silence to acknowledge the spiritual presence of (Names of the ones not present. Then tell how the person(s) influenced their life or how they loved their spouse or would have loved their spouse if they'd known them. This is a great opportunity to add something fun that can lighten the moment) Join me now for a moment of silence, please.

A Bit of Dazzle

[Couple's Names] have placed a small tree in the reception area where they've hung as ornaments the pictures of all those they wish could be here today but can't. (Here's where you CAN quickly mention their names only). We hope you'll take some time to see who they are and smile with [Couple's Names] at what wonderful people they are/were. On the back of their photos is something that very briefly tells what made [Couple's Names] love them so much.

2 ARCHWAY PRONOUNCEMENT

I love symbolism which is one of the reasons the Unity movement is my denomination of choice. I come from a Presbyterian background during a time when traditional religions were still growing, and mega-churches were barely beginning to make their mark on the church landscape. Weddings were traditional, and basically uniform, meaning no matter where you went, the wedding text was the same, the tone set, similar.

Going through ministerial school, we studied all kinds of spiritual practices and because Unity can be a bit on the woo-woo spectrum anyway, I got a chance to look more deeply into symbolism. Because my forte was ceremony, I created a rite of passage for young people growing from childhood into a teenager. The process involved walking through the frame of a doorway. One side of the doorway was their life as a child, and on the other, adulthood.

From a historical perspective, a wedding ceremony is a rite of passage. Many times, officiants conduct a ceremony within the frame of an archway that seems to be a good way to hold up masses of beautiful flowers. It frames the main focus of the ceremony but other than that it has little purpose. Unless of course it's windy and the arch hasn't been secured. In that case, it's a pain in the you-know-what to keep it in place.

But as a rite of passage, the arch is symbolic of a doorway. On one side is the past, living life one way and then transitioning through into another way of life, from being single and self-oriented to being married and dedicated to the other's well-being.

When I got the chance to officiate for a traditional, religious groom and a semi-woo-woo bride, I explained the symbolism of the archway. They loved the idea of walking through the doorway to further symbolize their new life and commitment to each other, so I created the following pronouncement ceremony which, BTW was very, very well received because it was unexpected and unique. I hope you'll give it a try and let me know how it goes!

Process

This takes place after the couple is pronounced married.

Officiant: "You may seal your vows with a kiss."

Everyone claps and goes crazy...

Script

Officiant: The archway behind us may look like a great place to display beautiful flowers. But it is also symbolic of a doorway. On one side of the doorway is [Couple's Names] old lives as single people. Even if they're living a life together it's been without the commitment they just made to each other.

On the other side of this archway, their new life as a married couple waits for them. By walking through this "doorway" they are further showing that they're leaving their old life behind and are instead entering into a new way of life together.

I now invite [Couple's Name] to walk through this door, ready to start their life together as [preferred roles such as husband and wife]. The couple walks through the archway and around to stand and face their friends and family. People go craaazzzzy yet again, clapping and laughing as the couple takes up their recessional down the aisle.

A Bit of Dazzle

When the couple has walked through the Arch and before the officiant introduces them by their married names, lead the guests in a cheer or affirmation such as "Welcome to your amazing future." "Live long and prosper" and for humor make the Dr. Spock / Star Trek hand symbol for live long and prosper.

3 BLANKET RITUAL

In the original, traditional Native American ceremony, each partner is wrapped in individual blankets, usually blue which represents their past, single lives. Next the Officiant gives a blessing and removes the blankets. The couple is then wrapped in a single white blanket. The white represents their new life, to be filled with peace and happiness. The white blanket is kept by the couple and displayed in their home.

Supplies
2 blue blankets or shawls can also be used
1 white blanket
Table to hold the blankets

Script
Officiant: In the Native American tradition wisdom and connection with the spirit world shows up in everyday life as well as special occasions. The tradition [Couple's Names] are about to enact is a representation of their past, single lives, represented by the single blue blankets, and then being transformed into a new life which they'll create together, symbolized by the beautiful white blanket.

Optional: Tell a story of why the couple chose any or all of the blankets, such as where it came from or who made it, and why that has meaning for the couple. If the couple chose colors that are not the traditional blue and white, is there a meaning behind the colors they chose? Colors have different meanings depending in the Native American culture. For the meanings of different colors in Native American lore, see the Links Directory.

The blue blankets represent wisdom and intuition, inspired by the flowing rivers, sun-kissed lakes, and abundant streams.

[Couple's Names] [Maid/Matron of Honor] and [Best Man] will place the blue blankets on them.

Optional: Anyone the couple designates can place the blankets around their shoulders and their relationship to the couple can be mentioned. The selected couple sets the blue blankets on the shoulders of Partner1 and Partner2.

Optional: The couple walks around the altar area or up and down the aisle. They should not hold hands. They return to the front and face the Officiant.

Officiant: It's our couple's desire to show the importance of joining their lives as one under the direction of the Spirit of all Life. This oneness is represented by the white blanket. White indicates their heart of sharing, purity, and light.

Option: The officiant or a grandparent, parent, or esteemed friend or family member wraps the blanket around the couple. If that person wants to give them a very short blessing this is also an option.

(The couple walks up and down the aisle or around the altar together.)

NOTE: Suggest the couple practice walking together wrapped in a blanket before the actual ceremony so they don't inadvertently cause a stumble. They don't have to be wrapped TIGHTLY together.

Officiant: Let the great Spirit that watches over you and moves through you show you the power of the love you have found, that you are a blessing to everyone you meet, bringing you an awareness of the purpose that brings you together in this marriage. May you live long in happiness and peace together.

Option: The couple may elect to keep the blanket on as they're pronounced married or they can have it removed and place the covering on the altar.

Modifications

This ritual can be easily modified to use just one blanket and choosing the blanket can also be part of the symbolism the officiant can emphasize as part of the meaning of the ceremony.

◆ ◆ ◆

A Bit of Dazzle

At least a week before the ceremony, ask the couple's closest friends/family members to gift them a small object, no bigger and definitely not heavier than a small skipping stone, that represents their best wishes for the couple. Examples are: a feather to represent freedom, a leaf to represent growth, a gemstone to show they value each other, creativity represented by a piece of embroidered fabric, or strength symbolized by a very small stone.

Place the objects in a pouch that's then sewn onto the edge of the white blanket. This is to remind them of the hopes their friends and family have for them. If there are fifty people or so, then invite the most important people to them to offer these gifts. These can be sewn onto the blanket after the ceremony but attaching the pouch to the blanket during the ceremony can be meaningful too.

4 BOURBON BLENDING

This is a unique ceremony that definitely takes pre-planning. What makes the ceremony meaningful is it's a metaphor for how our ability to love and grow gets better with age. Like so many special ceremonies, it's significant because of the many different ingredients that have to come together so the final outcome is worth the effort. It seems complicated, but when all the pieces come together it can be quite a fun ceremony because it has involved many people, and is interactive. These kinds of collaborative ceremonies are becoming more and more popular.

Considerations
Be sure to learn about the properties of the various whiskeys. Not all whiskeys complement each other. There's a great Whiskey Blending Wedding Guide at Whiskeymade.com.

If either of the mixed liquors interacts with sunlight, use a dark container.

Think about how often the couple will be drinking from the bottle. They need to decide if this will be something they'll do every year, every other year, every five years. If they plan on drinking from this mixture yearly, a larger receptacle will be required than if it's going to be an every-five-years arrangement as the liquor will be drained more quickly since it's used more often.

Supplies
10-liter barrel or large bottle for blending smaller amounts of whiskeys
Whiskey (such as corn mash, wheat, or rye)
Bottles for pouring the blended whiskey at the anniversary
Resource for barrels, whiskey, and bottles: See Link Directory.

Script

Officiant: Today [Couple's Names] are going to blend their lives together by the mixing of their two favorite whiskeys. Why? Because bourbon lasts much longer than beer or other spirits--and it gets better with age. Just like marriage.

This is a ten-liter barrel. At the rehearsal yesterday, [Couple's Names] and their family filled this cask (if applicable) with (type of whiskey such as corn mash, wheat or rye) and some added more into the cask prior to this ceremony beginning today.

Partially filling the cask yesterday is symbolic of the people who have brought you to today, to this amazing time here and now that you all share together.

[Couple's Names] are now pouring a complimentary whiskey(s) into the cask. [Partner1's] whiskey is _____ (example: Corn Spirit.) The whiskey [Partner2] is adding is _____ (example: Rye). These are the final ingredients to complete the mix that will age for a year so they can enjoy it on their first anniversary.

As you can see, clear alcohol is going in, but what will come out is something richer and much darker.

This mixture will take on the color of the oak of the barrel, not unlike the way your marriage will take on the color of your lives, your triumphs, goals that have been met as well as disappointments and mistakes.

The idea is for this mix to be a symbolic blending of the two of you and your experience of Spirit which you bring to your marriage. Likewise, Bourbon whiskey makes for an interesting symbolic substance. It's literally a blending of different spirits, that through mixing and aging together, combine to become something richer, more complex, and flavorful -- much like a good marriage.

Now that the liquor has been blended, [Couple's Names] will open the cask in one, two, or five years, depending on their restraint. They'll be reminded of this day and all who were here with them.

Couple steps back to their place for the pronouncement.

Option: The couple can also have participated in Bourbon Ceremony #2 and can drink from the whiskey they've dug up as the officiant pronounces them married. But most likely the bourbon would have been made months ahead of time.

A Bit of Dazzle

Close friends or family can contribute a beautiful cask to the ceremony to store the couple's whiskey in.

Engraving the cask or bottles for filling later is a great way to customize the ceremony elements. The best man and/or the matron/maid of honor can present the bottles or the officiant can point this out as part of the ceremony.

The couple can plan to renew their vows once the bourbon runs out!

The couple can bottle a portion of the bourbon and pass it on to their children who can, in turn, do this ceremony and start a new tradition. Starting new traditions that can be passed on from generation to generation can be a powerful statement of family.

Photo, Whiskeymade.com

5 BOURBON, KEEP THE RAIN AWAY

This ceremony is much easier to enact than the Bourbon Ceremony #1 because it's more practical and nothing needs to be blended, only purchased and buried (with permission). It too can be shared with everyone at the wedding.

Keep the Rain Away

Whether this is true or not, whiskey makers say if you take a bottle of bourbon and bury it at the couple's venue a month before their wedding, the weather will be rain-free. Then, on the day of their nuptials they dig up the bottle together as a part of the ceremony and share a glass together as the officiant pronounces them married or as a toast where they take their first sips together.

There are two ways to think of this ceremony as either s a tad superstitious or it proves the power of united minds to make something happen such as change the weather! It's a fun ceremony especially because many ceremonies are held outdoors and nature is one life element we cannot control. Here's a fun way to give controlling her a try. Resource: WhiskeyMade.com

Supplies

Shovel
Table
Cloth for cleaning off the bottle of Bourbon

Glasses for drinking and sharing the Bourbon

Script

Officiant: Whether [Couple's Names] are true born-and-bred Southerners or not, today we're completing the tradition of the Burying of the Bourbon. Today, as part of their ceremony, [Couple's Names] are digging up the bourbon.

The saying goes something like this: "Bury a bottle of bourbon a month to the day to keep the rain away."

A month ago, with the venue's permission, [Couple's Names] went through the following process: Made sure the venue wouldn't think they were grave diggers by digging the hole where they buried their bourbon.

Together, [Couple's Names] buried a bottle of Bourbon (may give the name and any history around this Bourbon) which they had carefully selected, placing the bottle in the ground upside down. The bottle was placed in the ground on a beautiful day to help ensure the same kind of beautiful day would be repeated the day the bottle was dug up.

Officiant: As you can see, burying the bourbon worked. Hence, the great weather we're having today!): As you can see, it worked. Hence, the great weather we're having today!

So now, I'm going to direct [Couple's Names] to dig up their buried Bourbon.

Process

Make sure the place where the Bourbon is buried is clearly marked.

The couple takes their shovel and together they dig up the bottle of Bourbon. Encourage everyone to cheer as they pull it out of the ground. The couple hands the bottle to the officiant who then cleans it off and places it on the table.

(Officiant opens the bottle and pours two small glasses for them to share.)

Officiant: We want to thank both of you for a beautiful day. It's not only important that the blending of the whiskeys made this Bourbon keep the rain away, but also this symbolizes the blending of your two lives into something better together than alone.

In honor of the commitment you've made to love and learn together, now is the time to share in the Bourbon that's been hidden in the ground getting ready for this most important day.

(Couple drinks the Bourbon. Hooting and hollering ensues.)

Officiant: I now pronounce you married.

Optional: Let's raise our glasses together. May you live long and happy and prosperous lives.

What to do if it rains?

Most experienced Officiants have had to help couples see the bright side when their outdoor wedding gets rained on. Some may brave the weather, others may move their ceremony inside.

Here are a few suggestions if this project seems to have failed:

- Emphasize the rain is just the beginning of a beautiful day to come Add some humor -- they needed to bury two bottles of bourbon instead of one
- The bourbon should have been buried for two months considering global warming
- Humor with truth: photos actually look great when the background is grey.
- Complement them for caring for their guests so much that they've put their plans aside so guests don't have to get wet. Even though they love their bourbon, it comes second to their guests
- Rain can be symbolic of fertility so please let us know when their little one is coming (be sure the couple is open to having children)

A Bit of Dazzle

The couple can save a portion of their bourbon and drink it as a toast when/if their first child gets married. Or buy a bottle for each child the couple plans to have and serve it at their child's wedding.

Bread photo courtesy of baker, Katya Lyukum

6 BREAD AND SALT

This Eastern European ceremony is usually done at the reception when the couple is first introduced to their guests as a married couple. I've combined both traditions in this ceremony and made it a bit more contemporary so it's not quite so Patriarchal. While the bread still symbolizes abundance, health, and longevity in both ceremonies, there is a bit of a different twist to each of them.

The Polish version uses bread in the hopes the couple will never go hungry or be in need. This version can be used either during the ceremony OR at the beginning of the reception, when the couple takes a piece of bread that's been pre-sliced and salted, drink the wine, and then throw the glass to the ground to break it.

While there are a few interpretations of the breaking of the glass, a few options for you to use in your ceremony are to emphasize the fragility of life, or by breaking the glass it's done in remembrance of past hardships where things break down. Difficult life experiences visit every couple but symbolically breaking the glass means the hardship has already happened so the future doesn't have to repeat the tragedy of the past.

In this version, breaking the glass is symbolic of the couple's breaking with their past lives so that they can create a new life and family together.

The Russian version is the same, however it's also a ceremony to determine who the head of the household will be. The couple is given a loaf of Karavai and someone holds the bread for them as they each take a bite from the loaf. Whoever takes the bigger bite is considered the head of the household. How about them apples? I didn't include this part in this ceremony but you can add it back into it if you or your couple prefers.

To see the Russian version of this ceremony enacted, Visit Bread and Salt Blessing on YouTube. See Links Directory.

Supplies
Baked Korovai Bread. For a Korovai recipe see Links Directory
Coarse salt in shallow container
Small glasses for wine or vodka
Tray on which to place the bread, salt and optional beverages on
Flexible container such as a bag, napkin, or special piece of fabric to smash the glass in

People Needed
The couple's parents OR a representative can be present like grandparents, aunts, or uncles, or godparents. Contemporary couples may choose a close friend or other family member. The main thing is to realize that this can be a recreation of an old tradition and making it meaningful is what's important.

Script
Officiant: Our couple is now going to participate in the traditional Bread and Salt Blessing with their parents!

This ceremony symbolizes prosperity, happiness, and affluence and is a way to celebrate [Couple's Names] cultural heritage, just as a wedding is a tribute to two souls joining together as one to enjoy life.

Officiant: The mother is the one who gave life to her family and she shows she approves of her son's/daughter's choice of his/her mate with Bread and Salt. She's here to welcome Partner1/Partner2 into the family and bless the newlyweds with a long and happy life.

The couple is now going to break off a piece of bread and show it to the guests. Bread is symbolic of the fullness of your future lives together. Like yeast has made the dough rise and expand, it's your family's hope that your love will rise and expand through the years.

This bread also symbolizes the hope of both the parents of both of you that neither of you will ever want for much, never go hungry, and always have enough.

Now you may salt your bread pieces.

(Bread is dipped in the cup of salt or the mother may sprinkle salt on the bread).

Feed your piece of salted bread to each other. (Much like what Western cultures do when the couple feed each other wedding cake).

Salt symbolizes that life will be difficult at times, but [Couples' Names] will learn how to deal with and handle their struggles. Adversity can make them grow stronger as a couple when they go through the hard times together.

It's also true that you may annoy each other just as it's annoying to have a good piece of bread over-salted. May this be the last time you will annoy one another. You should be so fortunate!!

(Parents pour wine into the two glasses.)

Officiant: Now take a drink of (kind of beverage).

NOTE: If vodka is used, it also has the identity of pride and national identity for Russians. But the latter can be adapted to mean identity as a couple.

As you drink this wine, you drink to the long life of your marriage. May it be sweet and intoxicating, and may your commitment to each other's well-being never waver.

(Once the couple has finished their wine, the glasses are put into a bag or napkin by the couple so they can be smashed.)

Officiant: Breaking these glasses is symbolic of [Couple's Names] breaking with their past lives so that they may freely go forward and create a new life and family together.

Final Blessing

Officiant: Life is a mystery. As you remain true to your commitment to love, to grow together, to see the best in each other, and be willing to see things from each other's perspective you will go forward together in ways that are new and exciting. May your love rise and bear with any annoyances if they happen, and open the way for a brighter future for all.

A Bit of Dazzle

In the Polish version, the couple announces a donation to a food bank is being made in honor of everyone at their wedding. This represents the couple and guests alike living in abundance, in health, and well-being.

"Rituals are how we step into our private field of dreams, a small Elysium all our own. Rituals are made not just for us, but for those we want to pass them on to." Andre Aciman

7 BREAKING THE GLASS

This ceremony is a relatively new tradition (since the 1950's it's been used in this form more extensively) for a Jewish couple. The origin of the ceremony comes from a German custom during the middle ages because of the power they believed the shards contained.

There are several accepted explanations of the meaning of the groom breaking the glass using his right foot. One states that the couple will remain married for as long as there are shards of glass that have been shattered. Hence the groom better stomp that glass into a million pieces.

Others believe breaking the glass symbolizes the destruction of the Temple in Jerusalem. It's also been said the practice is to remind the couple that life can and will bring them sadness and trials as well as joy and happiness.

There's always been something that hasn't quite made sense about this ceremony for me. Apparently, I'm not alone, but for different reasons. Some Jewish authorities don't like the custom because the Talmud says nothing can be destroyed for the sole purpose of destroying it. For example, a tree can't just be cut down and left; the wood has to be used for construction or firewood. So, the critics ask why was an expensive glass wasted and good wine squandered?

Examining this custom from a historical perspective, the ceremony takes on a much deeper significance.

In the middle ages, all German weddings were held outside on the north side of the synagogue. The corner of this side of the building contained a special stone called the Wedding Stone. When the ceremony concluded, the groom threw the glass filled with wine at the stone where it broke into many pieces. Why?

First of all, the glass filled with wine was blessed and thus imbued with the power of the Creator. In Jeremiah 4:6, God warns the prophet to flee for safety because He will bring evil from the North. By marrying on the north side of the temple, evil forces that came to hurt the couple were wounded and driven away by the glass shards, thus damaging evil before it could hurt the bride and groom. In short, they beat evil to the punch.

The mid-century Wedding Stone had magical designs such as stars and chalices, astrological signs, arches, etc. "Mazel tov" was written which means more literally, "May you have a good constellation." Or "May you be protected by the constellations in the heavens."

After the 19th century, the 5-pointed star or Shield of David was engraved on the wedding stones instead of magical stars, which signified being protected by David. In the center of the star was the word for God.

During the holocaust, most churches and synagogues were destroyed that had the magical symbols on the Wedding Stone but about eighteen remain.

The Shield of David was used in newer construction of synagogues and temples. Again, breaking the glass against the Wedding Stone meant being shielded against the devil and calling on the power of God to prevent the intentions of evil toward the couple.

Following are two ceremonies of Breaking the Glass. One uses a somewhat traditional explanation. The second ceremony is created using the ancient meaning but is similar as far as the ritual's process and elements.

This ritual is done at the end of the ceremony after the officiant/celebrant has pronounced the couple married. You can have either Partner1 or Partner2 break the glass with his or her right foot, or the couple can break the glass together.

Another note: The right side of the body represents our masculine nature, pure, powerful, or superordinate aspect of our being. The foot is representative of understanding, or another way to say this is the foot is what we stand on and takes us forward in life. Smashing with the right foot by the man (bear with me here this is symbolic not literal) is to consciously choose to protect and defend the family that's being created, to be sure of God's presence, and to take a stand to protect the couple from ruin, or feeling separated from their divine nature. This separation is another interpretation of the nature of evil rather than it being an actual entity.

Resource
Excellent YouTube exploration of the tradition—Why Break a Glass at Weddings?—Professor Shalom Sabar. See Link Directory.

Supplies

Wine Glass, medium size

Sturdy pouch big enough so that the glass in it can be smashed without shards flying out and causing any injuries or a silicon wrap can be used to prevent broken glass from doing damage.

Wine

Note: The officiant should make sure the glass is securely wrapped before the ceremony begins Silicon wraps are available online that can be used to prevent the glass shards from escaping, which is certainly understandable. We don't want anyone hurt. What's important is to understand the meaning of the ritual being enacted.

Traditional Script, Breaking the Glass #1

Officiant: I now pronounce you married (or your preferred pronouncement).

Before we start our celebration of [Couple's Names] marriage, Breaking the Glass at a wedding is a symbolic prayer and hope that your love for one another will remain until the pieces of the glass come together again, or in other words, that your love will last forever.

The fragile nature of the glass also suggests the frailty of human relationships. Even the strongest of relationships can disintegrate when not tended to.

Let's bless the wine: May there be joy and the rich exchange of love in your marriage.

(Couple drink the wine.)

Officiant: The glass then, is broken to protect the marriage with this prayer – May your bond of love be as difficult to break as it would be to put together the pieces of this glass.

(Direct one or both of the Partners to smash the wrapped piece of glass with his/her right foot. First Partner1 can smash the glass, then Partner2).

Officiant: Invite everyone to applaud as the Couple kisses to a cheer of "Mazel tov!" May you be protected by the constellations in heaven.

◆◆◆

A Bit of Dazzle

Before the glass is broken, the couple pass the glass around so it can be blessed by their guests. The officiant can add as the glass is broken, "As you've blessed this glass, it's your agreement to give this couple your support and encouragement to help [Couple's Names] keep their marriage strong. May the bond between last Forever."

8 BREAKING THE GLASS, HISTORICAL VERSION

Supplies
Wine Glass, medium size
Sturdy pouch or bag big enough so once the glass is placed inside, it can be smashed without glass flying out and causing any injuries
A stepping stone or large block of fashioned cement

Script
Officiant: I now pronounce you married (or your preferred pronouncement).

Before we get to dance and sing together to celebrate [Couple's Names] marriage, according to ancient Jewish folklore, they're going to enact the Breaking the Glass ritual.

The Talmud teaches never to waste anything, so this is something we'll do today so that nothing is broken in vain, nothing wasted.

We think of glass as fragile but just as it can be easily broken, it can also be a sharp weapon to protect and defend. But rather than think of broken glass as a weapon against something outside of ourselves, we think of it as a symbolic weapon that protects [Couple's Names] from shaming or blaming themselves when they make the inevitable mistakes that are normal in any relationship. Those mistakes can cause inner growth where weakness is transformed into strengths, despair into certainty, doubt into faith.

[Couple's Names] you are protected by the power of God who only sees the good in you, the love in you, and that you live your lives together as one, guided and protected by the shield of Divine Love. The star of David is also symbolic of the power of a love greater than what you now know to guide you into the deeper meanings of loving another human being, and make you bigger when you might have stayed smaller.

(The meaning of the wine. The power of one element (the grape) transformed into another (the wine) which can change our point of view on the world, hopefully for the better!)

Let's bless the wine: May there be joy and the rich exchange of love in your marriage. May all hurts be transformed by forgiveness, and all joy multiplied by your patience and passion.

(Officiant pours wine into the glass.)

Officiant (may hold the glass of wine up): Drink the wine now in honor of your transformation from two to one, uncertainty to clarity, chaos to peace. (Hands glass to the couple).

(Couple drinks the wine.)

(Officiant takes the empty glass and puts it in the large pouch or sturdy bag and hands it to the couple.)

Officiant: Rather than break the glass with your foot, today you are going to break the glass together against this block of cement to symbolize the many things that can get in your way in life.

The glass is broken against it to show you are protected in your marriage by God who loves and knows you, and shows you your path forward no matter what goes on around you.

Optional: Let's pray together – May [Couple's Names] be protected by the constellations in heaven, the power of God protect you, the Presence of God watch over you wherever you go, whatever you do for now and forevermore.

(Direct the Partners to smash the wrapped glass by hitting it against the block of cement or stone.)

Invite everyone to applaud as the Couple kisses to a cheer of "Mazel tov!" from the guests.

◆ ◆ ◆

A Bit of Dazzle

Decorate the cement stone with stars and goblets, and share how this type of stone was on the early temples when this ritual first began. A Bohemian couple could be the type of couple more likely to get behind the stars and rainbows. See the history that's detailed in the Introduction to this ceremony.

Photo by Rachel Claire from Pexels.com

9 CANDLE LIGHTING

This is a version of the traditional ceremony often used in Catholic weddings. It's also been used by couples who are no longer practicing Catholics. But they love the symbolism of two smaller lights becoming one bigger, brighter light just as they are more powerful as two individuals joined through marriage as one.

This ceremony is effective at the beginning of the nuptials but it can also be inserted after the couple share their vows to further emphasize leaving their single life behind and committing to the light within each other and making it brighter.

NOTE: This ceremony is not recommended for an outdoor wedding. Since officiants can easily have an ongoing battle between their script and the wind, it can take several tries, often unsuccessful, to light and keep the candle lit.

One option is to ask one or two of the attendants to stand against the wind while the candle is being lit and then quickly use a hurricane lamp to protect it as soon as any of the candles are lit.

When a flame goes out, some couples may take it as an omen that their relationship isn't going to work. So, help them not to overthink or read too much into a natural occurrence like the wind blowing a candle flame out! Be sure and read the story I wrote about my first wedding and ceremony. You'll understand why I make these recommendations!

Supplies

Two taper candles
One large candle
Candleholders
Table with covering
2 small and one large hurricane lamp cover if the ceremony is enacted outside (but DON'T DO IT!!)
Large wooden matches and case OR lighter. Check to make sure the lighter easily works.
Optional: Candle snuffer

Process

Have the mothers of the couple light their "child's" smaller taper candle either before the entire ceremony begins, or to signify the beginning of this special ceremony.

Script

Officiant: Marriage brings two people together in a very unique relationship. In this bond, you will share many experiences as if you're one person. You'll be there for each other and have each other's best interests in mind. Even as you often seem to be acting as one, both of you will always retain your own identity. The miracle of love is that it allows you to overcome any sense of isolation, yet continues to permit you your individuality.

[Couples Names], the two-lit candies symbolize your past, your separate lives, your separate families, and your separate sets of friends that you bring here today. But today, you're committing to make your family bigger by taking in each other's family and friends as your own, and to be brighter lights in a new future you'll build together as the days, months, and years unfold. Both of you may take one of the individual candles and then, together, light the center candle.

(Partner1 stands on one side of the table facing the congregation, and Partner2 stands on the opposite side of the table facing family and friends. They each take a smaller taper and light the larger unity candle together as they repeat after Officiant).

Officiant: Please repeat after me: May our love for one another ... continue to increase ... as our lights grow brighter ... May our days together be many and joyous ... and doubt or darkness cannot overcome us ... for we can depend on each other's love forever.

The merging of your two lights into the one light indicates your desire for your two lives, and the lives of your families and friends to be joined as one.

Now you may blow out your individual candles to indicate you are ready to leave your separate lives behind in the past and become a stronger force for good just as this one light shows us how bright you are as a couple. There's nothing you can't do together.

It's our prayer and dearest wish, that you'll keep these candles of love lit within your hearts, so there'll always be light and joy, peace and harmony in your home.

Couple return to their places and the ceremony proceeds.

A Bit of Dazzle
Do not blow out the individual candles.

Tell an anecdote: At a ministerial meeting a pastor told the story about a recent Candle Lighting ceremony he'd led where the couple elected to keep their individual candles lit after they'd joined their flames to symbolize their becoming one. Then the bride, an impish gleam in her eye, bent over and blew out her husband's candle. When Father Tom Glen heard of this he commented wryly, "During the marriage ceremony two become one – on the honeymoon they discover which one."

Dazzle Script
Officiant: You will never lose your individuality even though you are committing to a life well-lived together. You each have a life with your own passions and talents, but you're combining all you are into this relationship so your individuality is in service of your commitment to your unity.

10 FIRST ASSUMPTIONS

The first wedding ceremony I ever officiated took place on a humid Fall day in Atlanta, Georgia, in a tree-lined backyard belonging to the couple's family. Chris and Ken had hired me through the church.

To describe me as nervous would have accurately compared me to a leaf shaking in the wind. Even though my fellow students and I led mock weddings in ministerial school, I was excited to be leading a wedding while at the same time questioning whether or not I could really do this wedding thing. My strong suit in school was ceremony, not Bible, metaphysics, nor counseling, When I contemplated everything that could go wrong, I was already embarrassed by mistakes I hadn't even made yet.

During the week, I'd gone over and over my script. I felt fairly well prepared. Chris and Ken had hired me through the church. When I arrived at the house, I stopped the car and sat for a few minutes to calm myself with a few deep breaths. Finally, I opened the door, swung my legs out of the car, took one more deep breath, and with my ceremony text inside my small white binder said to myself, "Let's do this, Yarlott." My maiden voyage into ceremony was about to get underway.

Guests stood in the area where the ceremony would take place and were talking with each other. People looked over when I walked in, and without a smile or hello, they turned back to their conversations. I introduced myself to a woman in blue slacks and a green polo shirt and asked her where I could find the bride or groom. She nodded towards the back of the house and off I went.

Chris and Ken had asked me to do a Candle Lighting ceremony. I think doing this ceremony was to compensate for the fact that, as they put it, "We're Catholic, but we don't go to church." So as I made my way to the house, I looked for a table where the special ceremony would take place.

There was a plain square block about three feet high near a big vase of flowers. Fifteen feet away, thirty to forty white folding chairs had been placed facing the flowers, so I assumed this was the area where we'd stand. A napkin was plopped on top of the block, but I could see scuff marks, nicks, and black marks in the wood. There was no evidence of the things we'd need for the candle ceremony—no candle, no tapers, no candle holder, no matches—that we'd need to make the ceremony happen, just the block of wood.

I located Chris, and even though she was beautiful, she looked stressed and shaky. "Chris, where are the supplies for the Candle Lighting ceremony?" I asked. Her answer became the first lesson I learned by making a mistake in a ceremony—never assume anyone knows anything.

"I thought you were supposed to supply the candles and everything," she said.

"No," I answered. "This is something you should do because I don't know what you like."

This mistake went on a mental checklist: remind the couple they need to buy the elements for their special ceremony.

The ceremony was supposed to start in twenty minutes, so when I returned to the backyard, I grabbed a few of her friends. We looked around the house and pulled together a makeshift candle lighting ceremony made out of a pre-used pillar candle which we tied with a ribbon and bow, one new taper from a drawer in the kitchen, and a scented jar candle. We were good to go.

(Having the ability to improvise is a plus for an officiant.)

With everything in place, the ceremony began with Ken standing next to me in black jeans and a white shirt. Chris's uncle walked her down the aisle. I read my script, trying to sound natural but sure I sounded like I was reading a DIY manual. I knew I should look up now and then at the couple so I'd stick my finger where I left off, look into their eyes, and continue on. When we got to their vows (the traditional for richer for poorer) and they exchanged their rings, everything went perfectly.

The Candle Lighting ceremony went along fine if no one considered the fact that the flames blew out four or five times. We were outside, and the wind was low when we started the ceremony, but now, it had whipped up. Voila – lesson #2: never to do a Candle Lighting ceremony outside unless someone is equipped with excellent wind-management strategies. A hurricane lamp cover is a must, or numerous bodies willing to huddle around the candles so the flames don't go out if they need to stay lit for more than 30 seconds. We don't want anyone to think the flickers blowing out is an omen of their love going out, now do we?

We finally let the flames go out and I must've mumbled something about the love in their hearts could never go out. With that, I pronounced them married by holding my hand over their clasped hands. They kissed and walked back down the aisle. My first ceremony was over but there was one more lesson I learned that day, a triple hitter.

When we lead a ceremony at a couple's home the people who do the set up usually don't know the right distance to set the chairs up in relation to where the wedding party will stand. I was new and nervous. As a result, I didn't project my voice or even think about it because I was so distracted by everything else going on in my head. When I went out to the guests to say hello and attempt to soothe my pre-bruised ego, I asked a few how they liked the ceremony. "We don't know. We couldn't hear anything you said."

Ah…so make sure the distance between where the ceremony takes place and the couple is minimal when there's no microphone. And my rule of thumb now is with thirty people or more, I need a microphone. You'll have to figure that out for yourself.

My first wedding taught me how easy it is to make assumptions, but also that no problems are insurmountable. What was your first ceremony like? Email me your story at crystal@nmiwo.com. I'd love to hear from you!

Jess and Charles

11 CANVAS AND PAINT

This is a fun ceremony for an artistic couple. It's symbolic in a colorful way of the blending of each person's uniqueness with their partner to create something unique and hopefully beautiful. One of the couples I did this with had their initials printed on the canvas they used. This meant they always had their own identity underneath all the change and growth, trials and tribulations they would go through as a couple. Put this option on your list of A Bit of Dazzle.

Beware! You can imagine it could be a disaster if paint flies on a wedding gown or fancy tuxedo.

One solution is to have very thick paint which also prevents the paint from dripping or spattering in the wind. However, thick paint keeps it from blending in quite as well to form a unique pattern. In that case, encourage the couple to use paintbrushes to create a distinctive pattern.

Supplies
Several colors of thick paint in clear jars
Several sizes of paintbrushes
Canvas

Small easel
Table for the easel to rest on
Pan, plates, or trough to catch paint drips
Paper towels / Wet cloth to quickly wipe any spatters

Script

Officiant: Every marriage starts as a blank canvas and every day is a splash of color.

The blank canvas represents today, your wedding day, and a new beginning. The paint colors signify the experiences that lie ahead. Each color is a moment to be had. Colors of joy and sorrow, blessings and heartache. The colors are your milestones, your celebrations, tribulations, passions, and dreams.

They are the moments that become the days that become years.

The painted canvas will be a representation of the spiritual artwork of your marriage, and your everyday life together. It will be exactly what the two of you make of it.

There will be places on the canvas when the colors blend and mix, flow together and create a new color of experiences shared.

There will be places when the colors stay separate and stand out alone and independent...yet, still a complement to the bold colors nearby.

And there may be areas of contrast. Parts of the canvas may look dark or messy and not at all to your liking. Yet contrast is necessary to make other colors stand out.

Let there be blank and bare spaces where the mystery of your journey is yet to reveal itself.

However, when you step back and look at the canvas in its entirety, you'll see that it truly is "An Original Masterpiece" unlike anything you've ever seen before. Each color, contrast, shadow, and blending of hues is as unique and beautiful as [Couple's Names] love for each other.

You can come forward and let's see what happens!

Couple step up to the blank canvas.

Option: The couple can pour their paint at the same time or separately. If the paint doesn't combine, hand them paintbrushes to make unique patterns. Officiant: And so creating a masterpiece of marriage continues. Couple step back to stand with the officiant.

A Bit of Dazzle

Let the couple tell you who or what the different colors represent that they choose. One color can represent their work, another the
together means to them. When they pour the paint, the officiant can narrate what the colors mean.

12 CHILDREN'S CEREMONIES

Many people love to include their children in their wedding ceremony. While there's many, many ways to include them, here are a few you can give a try. These normally take place after the couple exchange their vows.

Children can get restless so it's an important conversation to have with the couple and ask, "Your children are wonderful kids. Do you have an idea of who they can go to or what you'll do if they get restless? Or is it okay with you if they make a fuss or are noisy? You know them much better than I do it is a good idea to have a plan in place so there's no guessing what should be done by whom, or be embarrassed."

Not all children are going to know what it means to" respect" or "honor" their step-parent so use words they'll be more likely to track with. Use "think your parents are really cool" or "pay attention to what they say." Let the child be playful as a way to consent or say "Yes" to any questions they need to answer.

Presenting the children with a gift such as a necklace, bracelet or something that reminds them of a special hobby or game they enjoy (like a box of Legos) can become a symbol of your commitment to your children and shows them you're paying attention to what's important to them. When you do this in public, it carries more weight because they're publically being acknowledged.

Children's Vows
Officiant: Do you [Couple's Names], take Child as your own, promising to love him/her and care for him/he, providing for his/her needs, both physical and spiritual?

Couple: We will. Do you [Child's Name] accept Partner2/Partner1 into your family? Do you promise to love and be happy with him/her as your step father/step mother?

Child: I do. NOTE: This consent can be repeated separately for each child, or led as a group "I do."

[Couple's Names], today you've promised your love to one another, and you've pledged your love to your child/ren as well. This commitment is beautiful and we are very happy that you're a family.

Optional: [Child/ren's Names] your parents have a gift for you as a symbol of their commitment to you, and to show you they trust and love you very much.

Gift is presented.

NOTE: If this simple ritual takes place near the end of the ceremony, then your couple should choose beforehand if they want to the child/ren to be present with them when the officiant makes their pronouncement of marriage. Otherwise the child/ren should be seated after they receive their gift and a hug from the parents.

New Sibling Vows

Officiant: [Child/ren's Names] you've always been the most important part of your dad and mom's life, and they are so proud of you. Today they're making a promise to one another. It's a promise that whatever may happen, good or bad, that they'll always be there for one another.

This promise is also a promise to you. You are already family. They love you with all their hearts, and no matter how big you get or where life takes you, they want you to know they promise to love you forever. They also want you to think of each other as brothers/sisters for life too. So, we're going to do something really fun. Are you game?

Child/ren acknowledge a yes.

Officiant: I'm going to ask you a very important question, [Child's Name]. Do you take [Sibling Name(s)] to be your brother/sister? If that's something you can do, say (choose one to present to the child/ren) "Yes" or "Indeed" or "I do!"

Child: "Yes."

Officiant: (To the other sibling), [Sibling Name], do you take [Child's Name] to be your brother/sister?

Child: "Yes."

Optional: The officiant may want to repeat this for each child or this can be done as a group from Partner1's children to Partner2's children.

Officiant: From today on you are officially brothers/sisters! Grow together, play together, share your mom and dad with one another, and know that you're going to have a great life together. God blesses your family always!

A Bit of Dazzle
Give the children drums, noisemakers, or streamers to wave in consent or celebration. You can also create a special dance or handshake, or simply give a high five as a way to accept the new parent or sibling.

13 COIN AND LASSO

This ceremony comes from the Romans, whose tradition included two "piles" of gold or silver coins into one half that's kept by the woman and the other half retained by the man as a pledge of their mutual support in their marriage.

Nowadays, las arras (Spanish for "The Coins" as a down payment), consists of thirteen coins substituted for the gold and silver of old. This is a very popular ceremony among Spanish, Filipino, and Mexican communities.

Symbolism

The thirteen coins denote the unconditional love between the husband and wife. Partner2 pledges to place all of his goods into his partner's care.

The passing of coins back and forth is a symbol of sharing worldly goods for richer or for poorer. Partner1 then gives back the coins to Partner2, promising confidence and dedication. These coins become one of the family heirlooms. The number thirteen represents the goods to be shared by the couple during the twelve months of each year, while the thirteenth coin is their promise to share their wealth with the poor.

When the Lasso is placed over the heads of the couple, the doubled rosary makes an infinity symbol which is also symbolic of the couple's union to each other and with God.

Supplies
13 coins
Suitable box to hold the coins
Table for the box and
Lasso Arras or Lasso

People Needed
A person important to the couple to present the coins at the beginning of the ceremony
Two sponsors, preferably a married couple well-known by the couple

Resources
Check Etsy and Link Directory for Lasso, Arras and Boxes
There are also YouTube videos showing how this ceremony is conducted

Process
On top of a table is the decorative box that contains the coins.

Alternative: A person who's important to the couple brings the box with the coins forward and gives it to the officiant.

Script
Blessing the Coins
Officiant removes the coins from the box and places them in Partner2's cupped hands.

Exchange of Coins
Officiant to Partner2: Please repeat after me: "Partner1, receive also these coins: they are a token of the care that I will have for you so that we will not lack what is necessary for us in our home."

Partner2 drops the coins in Partner1's cupped hands.

Officiant to Partner1: Please, repeat after me: "Partner2, I receive these coins as a token of God's blessing on us and a sign of the goods that we will share together."

Partner1 drops the coins back into Partner2's cupped hands.

Officiant: The thirteen coins are significant because they denote the unconditional love between the husband and wife. Partner2 pledges to place all of Partner2's goods into Partner1's care. The passing of coins back and forth is a symbol of sharing worldly goods for richer or for poorer. They make promises of confidence and dedication to each other. These coins become (or is) one of your family heirlooms. The number thirteen represents the goods to be shared by [Couple's Names] during the twelve months of each year, while the thirteenth coin is their promise to share their wealth with those who are underserved.

Exchange of Lassos
Presenting the Lassos by the Sponsors
Officiant: (Holds up the Lasso) This symbolic cord represents the commitment blessed by God that [Couple's Names] have promised each

other. The Arras/Lassos points to the life the couple will share as one. This life, imitating a Rosary, will be filled with joyful, sorrowful, luminous, and exciting mysteries. Invite Sponsors to be ready to present the Arras/Lasso to the couple. Blessing the Arras/Lasso Officiant: We know our Loving Creator is the wisdom that brought [Couple's Names] together in marriage and expresses through them as a love that grows daily. God's love will always be available to them no matter where they go or what they do. We pray they remember to ask for His help whenever there's a need, or just for the joy of talking with God.

Optional Reading–Romans 12

Sponsors are invited forward and stand before the couple.

Officiant: Now the symbol of unity with each other and God is placed around their necks.

Sponsors place the Lasso around the couple's necks.

Officiant: [Couple's Names], may the joining together with this Lasso, the Rosary of the always Blessed Virgin Mary, be an inspiration for both of you. Remember that the holiness needed to preserve this new family, like the family of God, can only be obtained through your mutual love and devotion. May the love and wisdom of those who have gone before you in a marriage that is healthy and happy be an example to you during your entire life together!

Contemporary/Non-religious Blessing

May combining your lives as represented by wearing the Lasso be an inspiration to you today, tomorrow, and forever. Remember your commitment to love one another is a spiritual endeavor, to see and call out the best in each other. Understand here and now that you won't always get your way! Ask questions of one another. Seek to see things from the other's perspective. Pick your battles wisely, not randomly.

Last but not least, may you be willing to ask for help from those who are good counsel so you become stronger through adversity, and find the deeper meanings of love always calling you forward.

Sponsors are seated.

Couple turn to face the officiant.

A Bit of Dazzle

Direct your couple to face their guests and read this quote:

*"Prosperity and abundance start in the mind. If you feel and
believe that they are part of your life, soon they will be."–Remez
Sasson Remez*

Sasson is an author, blogger, and the founder of Success Consciousness. He writes on self-improvement, positive thinking and inner peace. Remez is Argentinian name, Sasson, French.

The Lasso can be hand-made by the Sponsors or have some significance because of where it came from, who created it, its history, and how they can pass it on to their children.

14 CHRISTIAN CROSS

The Unity Christian Cross Ceremony is a beautifully visual ceremony for devout Christian couples. The cross is the major religious symbol that, for this ceremony, is divided into two crosses and three pegs that hold the sections together. When assembled, each section symbolizes the fullness of each partner who is coming together to become one with the Christ.

There's no particular place to insert this ceremony in your framework ceremony. It goes well at the start of the ceremony as it makes a statement that this couple is Christ-centered first and foremost. If conducted near the end of the entire ceremony, it's a reminder of how important their faith is in their marriage.

Resource
UnityCross.com (photo by permission)
Link to see the ceremony enacted on Pinterest in Link Directory

Supplies
Unity Christian Cross
Table and table covering

Process
One partner, usually the groom, places the outer cross in the wood base.

Partner1, usually the bride, places the more delicate cross on the inside. Three pegs are placed by the Officiant and the couple to secure the pieces together.

Script

Officiant: "Now we're going to celebrate this new union with a Unity Cross Ceremony."

NOTE: *The Couple should stand behind the altar so they don't have their backs to their guests.*

Officiant: [Couple's Names], the covenant that you are making today is a three-part covenant- Partner2, Partner1, and our Lord Jesus Christ. Through this commitment, from this moment forward you will both be together on your journey through life and you will never be alone. Throughout life, you'll experience much joy and happiness, victories, and many blessings. During these times, remember that the Lord is there to celebrate with you.

Officiant: You'll also experience times of tough decisions, sorrow, and defeat. These are the times that you'll need to remember that the Lord is also with you.

It's during these moments that He will be your strength, your rock, your refuge. He will be there to carry you both through whatever your challenge is, and He will never break covenant with you. You'll be able to turn to His Word, for He freely gives wisdom to those who ask. His Word is true and never changes. His Word is the same yesterday, today, and forever.

To demonstrate you're becoming one in this three-part covenant, you've chosen to assemble The Unity Cross.

This cross represents the faith of [Couple's Names] knowing that they place Christ first at the center of their marriage and trust Him to lead them on this new journey that they begin today.

Officiant picks up Partner2's piece of the Unity Cross and says:

Officiant: The outer piece of the cross represents you, Partner2. It is strong and bold. It represents your role as the leader and protector of your family. In the book of Ephesians, you're reminded to love Partner1 as Jesus loved the Church, totally and completely giving yourself for her.

Officiant hands the piece to Partner2 and he places his cross onto the base. Officiant holding Partner1's piece of the cross, says:

Officiant: In Genesis, the scripture tells us that woman was created from man. Partner1, the inside piece of the cross represents you. It's delicate and it's beautiful. It represents your many capabilities and how God created you with such intricate detail and how you fit perfectly inside the protection of Partner2, completing the sculpture and representing the two of you becoming one.

Officiant hands the inner piece to Partner1 and she places it inside the cross. Officiant picks up the three pegs and holds them in her/his hand.

Officiant: These three pegs represent the Father, The Son, and the Holy Spirit. They represent how the Lord holds together this covenant with His security and the completeness that only our Heavenly Father can give. We will insert the pegs completing the sculpture showing God's place in [Couple's Names] marriage.

(If applicable: At this time three pegs are placed into the Unity Cross -- the Officiant places the one at the top, Partner2 the one on her/ his side, and Partner1 the one on his/her side.)

Officiant: The Scriptures tell us that a three-stranded cord is not easily broken (Ecc. 4:12), Matthew 19: 5-6, "For this reason, a man shall leave his father and mother and be united to his wife, and the two shall become one flesh. So, they are no longer two, but one flesh. Therefore, what God has joined together, let man not separate."

Prayer

Officiant: God of love, we know you bless the marriage of [Couple's Names] and surround their relationship and their home with an ever-growing love. May they always be aware of Your presence and Your care in their lives.

And now, [Couple's Name]
May the grace of Christ attend you,
The love of God surrounds you,
And the Holy Spirit keep you.
Wherever you go, whatever you do, whoever you become, all is well.
Amen.

Couple returns to their places in front of the officiant.

A Bit of Dazzle

If there's a program the couple has printed, include Matthew 19: 5-6 and ask the guests to repeat it with you as a community blessing to the couple.

> *Matthew 19:5: For this reason, a man shall leave his father and mother and be joined to his wife, and the two shall become one flesh. 6 So they are no longer two but one flesh. What therefore God has joined together, let not man put asunder.*

15 DIVORCE CEREMONY

Both marriage and divorce rates in the United States declined from 2009 to 2019 but rates vary from state to state according to the US Census Bureau.

It's interesting to note that of the 40% to 50% of marriages that end in divorce, the average marriage lasts about eight years. This statistic is counted from the time of filing for divorce, so this data does not include how long divorce attorneys might battle it out before officially filing. This is according to the It's Over Easy--48 Divorce Statistics in 2020 report.

> ~ In general, the time periods in which a couple is most likely to get divorced are the first two years of marriage, or in years five through eight.
> ~ Boomers now represent the age group most likely to divorce, with more than forty percent of couples aged 60+ divorced as of 2010.
> ~ According to marriage and relationship studies by Bloomberg News, millennials are staying together more than the previous generations were willing to.

The three big reasons? This is probably no surprise, but it's money, infidelity, and issues with sex. Some people can learn and grow their way through those problems together, and some can't, don't know how to, or won't.

Divorce does not have to be the end of the world. It can be the springboard into a new life that can prove to have been the best and most difficult experience that ever happened to a couple. To help clean up some of the messes created by resentments, betrayals, neglect, and a host of other negatives, the Divorce Ceremony may be an option.

This ceremony was created by the Reverend Judy Grimes of Unity School and Northern Michigan Ministers in Boyne City, Michigan. For a visual of a different Divorce Ceremony, visit *Grayson Perry: Rites of Passage* on YouTube. It's quite an amazing process this couple goes through, and obviously only for people who have a good level of maturity.

As the officiant directing this ritual, you should provide the couple with directions to write down the negative emotions--fears, guilt, resentments, pain, sadness—in a letter that they will burn at the ceremony. Rice paper is preferred because it doesn't smoke the way regular paper does.

Supplies

Music appropriate for new beginnings (Google for suggestions)
Burning Ritual materials
Two small tapers
Candle holders
Matches or lighter
4 x 10 sheets of rice paper (burns cleaner than wood-based paper)
Writing materials
Wok or bowl to burn the letters in that won't melt or burn
Wedding rings
Separate rings, necklaces, or other gift to give to children, if desired

Script

Officiant: [Couple's Names], we're here today to share in a cooperative act of dissolving the union of two people who have decided to walk different paths.

We participate in many ceremonies throughout our lives. Some are joyful and happy, some are filled with awe and wonder, while others may be filled with sadness and grief.

Yet all of these ceremonies are rites of passage—transitions from one state of being to another.

Today, we're participating in a rite of passage from a state of union to a state of separation. We want to make this passage as gentle as possible without denying the pain that each of you may be feeling.

You've taken legal steps to divide into independent persons. You're now ready to walk paths that can pave the way to a new, free-standing relationship that can have very special qualities of respect and communication.

Is this true, that you desire your separate paths to have the qualities of respect and communication?

Couple: Yes.

Each of you is ready to find a new sense of purpose that is truly your own. But in order that you may do this successfully, it's necessary to begin the process of releasing the past, the old hurts, fears, frustrations–and negative thoughts and emotions that might block your heart from moving forward.

When a separation takes place, deep roots are pulled apart. This can sometimes cause deep distress, pain that is often accompanied by questions that have no answers, and by feelings of guilt, doubt, and fear.

These feelings are real and they don't need an explanation but they need to be validated by providing comfort, support, and above all, love.

We gather also to lovingly support [children's names]. We have to tend to the hearts and minds of those who have little choice in the matter. Today, we'll also share this process of healing with them.

Burning Ritual

Officiant: Divorce is neither a right nor wrong decision. It's a choice. We're given not only the ability to choose but the responsibility to pick the path that will lead to our highest spiritual good and the full expression of our potential.

We don't always choose a path that is free of pain, and we don't always remain on the path we once chose.

As our spiritual unfolding continues, we know that we are doing our best, or else we would have done otherwise. We make mistakes, but that means we are choosing life and are willing to take risks.

[Couple's Names] you've each given this some thought and written these barriers to happiness on sheets of rice paper so that they may be symbolically released in the cleansing fire.

Is this so?

Couple: Yes, it is.

Officiant lights two single taper candles. Note: If this ceremony is done outdoors, you may want to keep it simple and use matches only.

Officiant: You have the ability to restore peace and harmony to your lives. When you forgive yourself and each other, you can gain new freedom through letting go of the past. Through forgiveness, you learn and progress. You keep the memories of what was good and the wisdom of lessons learned together.

You also acknowledge the pain and struggle. As you set the paper on fire, you change its substance from one form into another. The burning is symbolic of the transformation of your lives from a married couple back into two individuals.

Couple steps to the wok or fire bowl where two tapers have been lit or another type of candle.

[Couples Names], please light your paper and as it burns, repeat after me,

"In the Spirit of Truth ... I'm free ... and you're free."

Take time to pause and watch the smoke disappear. These ashes will be divided up and planted at the base of a new tree that [Couple's Names] are planting in each of their yards to symbolize the new growth that is taking place.

Ring Ceremony

Officiant: Although this ceremony commemorates the day of your divorce, your relationship doesn't end. There can never completely be a separation between you. For always there is a past that's been shared. Always there will be concerns of the present. Certain bonds remain between you.

And certain bonds must be broken in order to go forward. Are you ready to break these bonds?

Couple: Yes

Please repeat after me.
[Partner1] I hereby affirm my place ... in the ending of our marriage.
[Partner2] I hereby affirm my place ... in the ending of our marriage.

[Couple together] Now I enter into ... a new relationship with you. I treasure the beautiful things we have shared. I desire only good for you (and our children).

Above all ... I promise to respect you ... as an individual. This is my pledge.

Officiant: Please take out your rings. *Pause.*

Please give your rings back to each other.

Optional Prayer: Let the return of these rings be a release from a pledge once undertaken and now outlived. What this couple exchanged to keep is now returned, so may they be free to enter into a new life, separate now, not with regret for what was not achieved, but with hope and belief in what is yet possible. Amen.

And so, as you have both stated to one another, it is your intention to live apart and to create lives independent from one another. As you have further declared, you have a common commitment to respect yourself and each other.

I now pronounce your marriage dissolved. I summon your friends, family, and strangers to honor the decision you have made and the separate paths you have claimed.

Children's Ceremony
Officiant invites the children to come forward and stand between the parents.

Script
Officiant: This separation is in no way your responsibility; it is only something that your parents have decided to do because they want what's best for everyone. Your presence in their lives remains most important. You brought joy to their lives when you were born and you continue to bring them joy.

Officiant can lead each partner in the following as each refers to the other partner. Or you can provide a written copy they can read to the child separately.

[Partner2]: [Children's names], I am and always will be grateful for you. Nothing can ever erase my love for you, even though your mother/father and I have chosen to live apart. I give you this ring as a symbol of how much I love you. It has no beginning and no end. Such is my love for you (kiss).

[Partner 1]: [Children's names], I am and always will be grateful for you. Nothing can ever erase my love for you, even though your mother/father and I have chosen to live apart. I give you this necklace/chain as a symbol of the bond of love we share. Each link is a symbol of a happy and beautiful moment we have had together.

(Kiss)

Repeat for each child. Other symbolic gifts can of course be given such as flowers or saplings.

Optional Prayer

Officiant: Let's pray. May all that is noble, lovely, and true, all that is enriching and creative, and all that is beautiful be abundantly in your lives and bring peace and joy in your homes forever. Amen.

This concludes our service.

Note: Any part of this ceremony can also be done by one partner. For more unique rituals, see *Transformative Rituals: Celebrations for Personal Growth* by Gay and David Williamson. Available on Amazon.com.

A Bit of Dazzle

As barriers to happiness are released, if someone has a brass or crystal bowl that can be sounded, the tones can raise the vibration higher and ease sadness. Example: Sound the bowl after the Burning Ritual has taken place. Use the bowls again when the Ring Exchange has completed, etc.

> *"You've got to know the rules to break them. That's what I'm here for, to demolish the rules but to keep the tradition." Alexander McQueen*

16 FISHERMAN'S KNOT

I've done many Fisherman's Knot Ceremonies over the years and love the history behind it and the symbolism. Usually, it's the couple that loves the water in some capacity who elect to do this ceremony.

A Bit of History

During long fishing trips, the fisherman would create different knots and practice tying them. Some of the knots were decorative and others functional. As the script tells, the Fisherman's Knot was the tightest knot there was and never unraveled. It only got tighter as more stress was put on it (meaning that the more trials you go through in life will bring you and your mate even closer).

Traditionally this ceremony is enacted after the couple shares their vows but of course can be done wherever you think is best.

Learn how to tie a Fisherman's Knot on YouTube

Script

Officiant: [Couple's Names] have just sealed their relationship with the giving and receiving of rings. Today their relationship is further symbolized by the tying of a Fisherman's Knot, a true lovers knot, for it is the strongest there is; its bond will not break, becoming ever stronger under pressure.

[Couple's Names], will you please take the cords that will make your knot?

Couple take their cords off the table or from the easel where the cords are placed.

Officiant: These two cords represent your past; each of you as individuals and the unique and special gifts you bring to your marriage. As you fasten your pieces together, these actions represent the present, this moment when you join your two lives into one common purpose.

Couple ties the cord/rope together into the Fisherman's Knot.

Officiant: The completed knot represents your future, secure in the knowledge your relationship will continue to be strong despite the inevitable changes life brings. Although the fisherman's knot is one of the simplest to tie, it is also one of the sturdiest. As stress is applied, the knot becomes ever stronger.

It's the goal of marriage to achieve a blending of hearts and lives, but like the spaces between these cords formed by the knot, let there also be spaces in your new life together, so each may encourage and nurture the individual growth of the other.

Pull on this rope to see it strengthen under pressure while still allowing us to see the individual cords, just as your support of one another as beautiful and blessed individuals strengthens your union.

Couple pulls the rope together.

Officiant: As you hold one another in mutual concern and shared respect, may you continue holding each other tightly in your hearts and form a strong bond, now and forever. Let this knot indicate the strength of your love and be a symbol of your unity from this day forward.

A Bit of Dazzle

This is an opportunity for the couple to hang different mementos on the joined cord before they use it. The officiant might mention these items in the script for more meaning and depth.

17 FLOWER PRESENTATION

When a couple wants to acknowledge how important their parents have been in their lives, they may want to show their parents how much they appreciate them. Whenever I've set the following ceremony up for a couple, it's resulted in a touching and heartfelt moment.

Another way to consider the meaning of this ceremony is that it's symbolic of couple emphasizing that getting married is also a letting go of their childhood and saying goodbye to dependence on their parents. Choosing to present their parents (grandparents or others) with roses (or other flowers) during the wedding service is a sign of respect and recognition of their love and support for the people who have so consistently loved and supported them.

Set up

The flowers may be placed on the altar prior to the ceremony or held by a member of the wedding party and given to the couple at the appropriate time. Any color may be used although yellow continues the theme of sharing the light of love with others. Refer to the meaning of colors from the links in the Link Directory.

Discover the meaning of different colors of roses and flowers other than roses, and their symbolic meaning, see Flower Symbolism in the Link Directory.

As the couple presents the flowers to the parents, officiant chooses Option1 or Option2.

Option 1

Officiant: The love that [Couple's Names] feel for one another is the flowering of a seed their parents planted in their hearts years ago. As they embrace each other in their love, they also embrace their families, who have been brought together on this very special day. As a sign of their love for their families, [Couple's Names] would like to offer these symbols of their love, these roses, to their (mothers or fathers), NAME and NAME. These flowers are a promise that you are always in their hearts and prayers.

Following the presentation of the flowers, the couple return to their place with the officiant.

Option 2

Officiant: [Couple's Names] present these roses (flowers) to their parents (others) with affection and appreciation for the love and support that have brought them to this day.

Following the presentation of the flowers, the couple return to their place with the officiant.

A Bit of Dazzle

Attach a letter of appreciation or a charm from both Partner1 and Partner2 to the flowers. Make sure the mothers know the letter is in place.

18 GLASS BEAD

This ceremony is very similar in meaning to the Sand Ceremony. The Glass Bead ceremony further symbolizes transformation by creating a work of art that's visual in a more refined way than sand being poured into a jar.

The couple needs to arrange with a glassblower prior to the ceremony what they want the glass beads to become. They have to be mindful of the amount of glass beads they plan to combine. The more beads the bigger or thicker what they create can be. Options are to create a bowl, vase, paperweight, decorative ball, or a piece of jewelry.

This ceremony is a colorful alternative for couples who want a memento from their wedding ceremony that's more functional and decorative than a jar of sand on the mantle or in the cabinet.

Resource
Glass beads on Etsy: Unity Ceremony Keepsake Blown Glass Piece
See Link Directory

Set up

Note the colors of glass beads the couple is using and you can further symbolize the meaning of combining the beads by color. If the couple has decided what the glass beads will become, you can also incorporate this fact into the ceremony.

Script

Officiant: [Couple's Names], your marriage not only joins you together as a couple, it also joins your two families together in very unique and special relationships. It's important to know you have people you can share celebrations and times of loss and grief with but never lose your own identity. The miracle of love is that it allows you to overcome any sense of isolation, yet continues to encourage your individuality.

The ceremony you're about to engage in has two levels of meaning. First, we acknowledge that glass is fragile. Yet we know when we handle glass carefully, it lasts and lasts. The intensity of glass is very difficult to dull or diminish. Glass is amazingly beautiful and treating it with care means it will be preserved, be stunning when the light shines through it, and can be admired by those who see it.

Likewise, your marriage, when handled with care will bring great beauty into your life. Your relationship can be a joy for others to see. The depth of the love you've found truly makes the world a more beautiful place.

The second level of meaning in this ceremony lies in the two colors of glass beads you've chosen. These two colors symbolize your separate lives and your separate families that you bring here today. The merging of these glass pieces into one symbolizes your desire for your lives, your families and friends to be joined as one. The pattern you create will be unique, unlike any other, just like your love is like no other.

Invite the couple to the table.

You may now take your beads of glass and pour them together into the large single container.

Glass pieces are poured.

Officiant: When this special day is over, and you begin your new life as a married couple, you will take this container of mixed glass to a glassblower. S/He will create a bowl/ball/glass/vase out of what you've just blended as a reminder of the fragility, wonder, and beauty of your love and of this day.

We know that it is the wish of everyone here that you will continuously blend your families with love, sharing, and happiness so that there will always be light and joy, peace and harmony in all of your hearts and in your home.

Couple return to their place with the officiant.

A Bit of Dazzle

Some glassblowers can also incorporate a charm or object into their creation. As the officiant, you could gift a rose crystal, amethyst, or another semi-precious gemstone (we have Petoskey stones in my area) perhaps in the shape of a heart that can be included in the glassblower's creation.

Another option is to encourage one of the flowers in the bouquet to be dried and incorporated into the design.

19 HANDFASTING CEREMONY

This symbolic Unity ritual usually involves fastening a couple's hands together with cording, ribbon, twine, or a silk sash. Couples can opt to use a single strand or braid three strands together to represent the intertwining of the two individual lives into one. Generally, four to six feet in length, the cords can contain any color or made of any material flexible enough to wrap around the couple's joined hands.

The ceremony is from an early Celtic ceremony. It's where the expression, 'tying the knot' came from. Later on, the Irish, Scots, and the Welsh also adopted this ritual. It involves the tying of hands together to symbolize the coming together to serve one another and remain tied or joined together body, mind, and soul.

Note: While I've done my best in most ceremonies to be gender neutral so none of the ceremonies seem written only for heterosexual couples, this one from my original had so many changes to make that it seemed cumbersome to include all the his/her, s/he's that would have been necessary. It's not my intention to offend. But that's why you won't see this ceremony as particular with its nouns.

Supplies
One cord about five feet long or six cords, each about three feet long.

Numerous online wedding vendors sell ready-made and custom hand fasting cords.

Script

Officiant: Greetings friends and family and welcome to this day of celebration. We're here to witness the marriage of [Couple's Names]. We've been invited to share in the commitment they make to each other today. And we're happy to accept that invitation, yes? [Invite a yes from friends and family.]

If life has any meaning to us at all, it's because of the power of love. Love enriches our lives as human beings. It's the reason for peace in the family and peace on Earth. Of all the people on the planet, that these two met and chose to love each other is a beautiful miracle.

[Couple's Names] understanding of the true meaning of marriage has come alive from many influences; their families, their friends, and each of their own personal beliefs. We're here not only to strengthen the bonds of [Couple's Names] love for each other but also to bring family and friends together to celebrate these same bonds that hold us all together.

What defines [Couple's Names] love today will change and grow as life adds texture and color to their relationship. It takes seconds to say I love you, but it can take a lifetime to show it. This ceremony is the celebration of a new stage in a much larger process that's the love that continues to grow between two people who are realistic about the ups and downs in a relationship.

To the couple: The promises you will make today and the ties that are bound strengthen your union. They will cross the years and lives of your soul's growth.

Officiant: Do you seek to begin this ceremony?

Couple: "Yes we do."

Officiant asks the couple to look into each other's eyes.

Officiant to Partner2: Will you cause her pain?
Partner2: "I may."

Officiant to Partner2: Is that your intention?
Partner2: "No."

Officiant to Partner1: Will you cause him/her pain?
Partner1: "I may."

Officiant to Partner1: Is that your intention?
Partner1: "No."

Officiant to both: Will you share each other's pain and seek to ease it?
Both: "Yes."

Officiant to both: And so the binding is made. Join your hands.

The first cord is draped across or one cord is wrapped around Partner1 and Partner2's joined hands.

Officiant to Partner1: Will you share Partner2's laughter?
Partner1: "Yes."

Officiant to Partner2: Will you share Partner1's laughter?
Partner2: "Yes."

Officiant to both: Will both of you look for the brightness in life and see what's positive about each other?
Both: "Yes."

Officiant: And so the binding is made.

The second cord is draped across or one cord is wrapped around the couple's joined hands.

Officiant to Partner1: Will you burden him?
Partner1: "I may."

Officiant to Partner1: Is that your intention?
Partner1: "No."

Officiant to Partner2: Will you burden her?
Partner2: "I may."

Officiant to Partner2: Is that your intention?
Partner2: "No."

Officiant to both: Will you share the burdens of each so that your spirits may grow in this union?
Both: "Yes."

Officiant: And so, the binding is made.

The third cord is draped across or one cord is wrapped around the couple's joined hands.

Officiant to Partner1: Will you share his dreams?
Partner1: "Yes."

Officiant to Partner2: Will you share her dreams? Partner2: "Yes."

Officiant to both: Will you dream together to create new shared realities?
Both: "Yes."

Officiant: And so the binding is made.

The fourth cord is draped across or one cord is wrapped around the couple's joined hands.

Officiant to Partner2: Will you cause your partner anger?
Partner2: "I may."

Officiant to Partner2: Is that your intention?
Partner2: "No."

Officiant to Partner1: Will you cause partner anger?
Partner1: "I may."

Officiant to Partner1: Is that your intention?
Partner1: "No."

Officiant to both: Will you take the heat of anger and use it to temper the strength of this union?
Both: "We will."

Officiant: And so, the binding is made.

The fifth cord is draped across or one cord is wrapped around the couple's joined hands.

Officiant to Partner1: Will you honor him/her?
Partner1: "I will."

Officiant to Partner2: Will you honor her/him?
Partner2: "I will."

Officiant to both: Will you seek to never give cause to break that honor?
Both: "We shall never do so."

Officiant: And so, the final binding is made.

Drape the sixth cord across the couple's hands, and tie all cords together.

Officiant: The knots of this binding are not formed by these cords but instead by your vows. Either of you may drop the cords, for always you will hold in your own hands the making or breaking of this union."

As this knot is tied, so are your lives now bound. Woven into these cords, into its very fibers, are all the hopes of your friends and family, and of yourselves, for your new life together. With the entwining of this knot, do I tie all the desires, dreams, love and happiness wished here in this place to your lives for as long as love shall last.

In the joining of hands and the fashion of a knot, so are your lives now bound one to another. By this cord, you are thus bound to your vow. May this knot remain tied for as long as your love shall last.

May this cord draw your hands together in love, never to be used in anger. May the vows you have spoken never grow bitter in your mouths.

Two entwined in love, bound by commitment and fear, sadness and joy, by hardship and victory, anger and reconciliation, all of which brings strength to this union. Hold tight to one another through both good times and bad and watch as your strength grows. Remember that it is not this physical cord, but what it represents, that keeps you together.

Once the cords are tied together they can be removed if there's more of the entire ceremony to follow, and set them where they can be seen. Be sure they're removed so the couple can move easily as they seal their vows with a kiss.

A Few Bits of Dazzle
Let the Partners decorate the cord with feathers, beads, jewels, beach glass, pendants, charms, etc. before they're wrapped around their hands. They can share the reason the items they've chosen have significance for them. Or the officiant can explain for them as part of the ceremony.

Alternatively, the couple can also include specific gemstones or charms to bless the marriage which can also be included in the ceremony begins. For example, when the fourth cord is bound, a ruby* is attached to the cord, and the Officiant can say, after their declarations "Let this ruby remind you of your intention to create new shared realities." Or with the fifth binding, "Let this Larimer** remind you of your intention to temper the strength of this union."

* Rubies are often associated with wealth and prosperity. Many ancient crowns were decorated with rubies because they represented good fortune and courage. The ruby's deep red color also has ties to love, passion, and raw emotion. These are the foundations of many couples' dreams.

** Larimer is said to enlighten and heal in a physical, emotional, mental, and spiritual way. It stimulates the heart, throat, third eye, and crown chakras facilitating inner wisdom and outer manifestation. It represents peace and clarity radiating healing and love energy. It is recommended for people who are stressed.

20 RINGING OF THE CHIMES

The bride was parking the green minivan in our church parking lot. Standing in my doorway was the groom, Frank, and his big, toothy smile and long nose poked out from under his weathered, broad-brim leather hat. He hesitated before he came through the door, but I waved him into my office.

"Come on in," I said, and offered my hand. He took it and shook it like I was a man.

I liked him right away.

"Cherie's parking the car," he said, and then started to chatter about the weather and the drive in to town. He seemed a tad nervous and I knew he probably had some jitters that come with meeting anyone new, but especially a minister. He certainly wasn't the first to wonder what to make of me.

Cherie sauntered in. She was a solid woman who stood two inches taller than Frank. She had a round European face, and large square shoulders that looked soft in her oversized t-shirt. When she raised her arm to hug his neck, her shirt fell back and a tattooed star peeked out on her shoulder.

When he reached to return her hug, he bumped her arm, and the pile of papers I recognized as the wedding packet I had provided got knocked out of her hands and onto the floor. She smiled sideways at him and shook her head as if she'd been part of this scenario before. He apologized and smiled back. A good start for a couple, I thought, tolerance for whatever the moment brings.

"I'm so glad you could come," I told them, smiling. I wanted to put them at ease with a little pre-wedding meeting cheerfulness. "Please, sit on the couch."

Against the wall was a simple loveseat covered with an ill-fitting slipcover that I hoped didn't look as cheap as the couch it covered. I nodded in the direction of the loveseat and smiled. She slid into place, snug against the arm of the sofa. Frank plopped down next to her, all feet and arms. I took my seat opposite them at my desk.

Frank and Cherie were nature lovers, not the Thoreau kind, but the type of people who respect the outdoors because it provides game to hunt and plants for food. They told me they killed a deer this past season.

My first impression was these life mates fit into the opposites attract category because of her calmness, his exuberance; her height, his compact stature. I'd seen the yin yang pairing many times before. The introvert falls for the extrovert, the artist for the CPA, the demure succumbs to the projected strength of the controller. At the same time, they conveyed a deep love and respect for one another. Opposites can have more internal resources to help them weather the storms normal to any relationship, balancing extremes like drought and flood.

"We're looking for a minister who understands we want a different kind of ceremony," she said. "We really love to be outdoors. And we don't want anything in the ceremony that's too traditional." Frank nodded his head in agreement, and looked back and forth from her to me, from me to her. She smiled.

"I've been going to this place on the river for a bunch 'a years," Frank said, and nodded to Cherie.

"It's so pristine, we love it," Cherie added. "It's southeast, passed Fife Lake, on the Manistee River. We want to get married in the river."

They looked at me with similar soft smiles, a tease pursing their lips together. The message they were trying to give me hadn't yet sunk in.

"Lots of couples want to get married on the water," I assured them. "A vast majority of the weddings I officiate for are on the beach."

I thought I saw a twinkle in Frank's eyes. "We don't mean on the water's edge." He paused, and looked endearingly at Cherie. "We mean IN the river."

Silence. "What do you mean, IN the river?" I knew what he meant but I needed a minute to process what was coming. I'd heard of people wanting to get married on skis or horses because the sport is what drew them together. I even saw one wedding take place as the couple parachuted from a plane. There was no question I would never be doing THAT kind of a ceremony, but in the river?

"There's a spot in the river that's shallow, but you have to wade through deeper water to get there," he explained. "Do you have water shoes?"

"No.... So, you actually want to be IN the water when you exchange your vows?" The word IN stuck in my throat.

"Yes, this place means a lot to us. It's so beautiful."

How could it not be beautiful, I thought? The area we all lived in is surrounded by lakes, I understood their love of the water – I loved the water, too. The blue reflected from the sky, the glitter on the waves, the soft serenity of the waters is the primary reason I feel so fortunate to live near water.

"Well, I'm game," I said. "It might be, mmmm, very interesting."

"Great! Then we'd love to have you be our officiant!"

The rest of our meeting was fairly typical: finding out who was in their wedding party, what vows they wanted. I promised to send them a Celtic-based Hand Fasting Ceremony where the phrase, "tying the knot" came from.

The last thing I asked them was, "Do you have a plan B in case the weather is bad?"

"No. We have no plan B. The weather will be fine," they promised me.

Those were dangerous words in wedding land. One should always have a Plan B.

On the day of the wedding, the scowling weather was nasty and announced a chilly Fall was here. Dark rain clouds ruled out the sunny conditions every wedding couple hopes for. Temperatures dropped fifteen degrees from the high heat of just a few days ago. The night before, the rain was fierce. It drenched the land and created pockets of mud on dirt roads and walkways. In the sandy areas, the water drained away, but the surrounding grasses were pounded down and filled with rain that didn't have anywhere else to go.

Cherie had called me the day before the wedding, but I couldn't get back to her until 11:00 that night. I hadn't had a chance to look at the weather forecast, but I had a feeling it wasn't good. Her voice was groggy when she answered the phone. "The weather is supposed to be awful tomorrow: cold, raining, grey all day. Can you do the ceremony on Monday instead? All of our people are able to wait until Labor Day, if it's okay with you."

Unfortunately, it wasn't okay with me. Every year on Labor Day the state opens up the Mackinac (pronounced mack-in-awe) Bridge that connects the Upper Peninsula to the rest of Michigan. One half of the bridge allows approximately 50,000 pedestrians to walk the five miles across the Bridge. For the past twelve years, I was one of those thousands, and planned to do it this year.

"Monday won't work for me," I told her. "I won't be in town. I'm walking the Bridge."

"Well, then we'll just go ahead on Saturday."

"Isn't there someplace else you could get married that's inside?"

"No…No, this place really means a lot to us," she said calmly and deliberately. I could tell from her tone of voice she was not going to budge. The only tactic I had left was pulling rank. I was the minister. No me, no wedding. It took me two seconds to choose their hopes for their wedding day over my own discomfort.

"Okay. We'll go ahead then."

She thanked me, and assured me everything would work out fine. The truth was that many bad weather weddings I'd done had a magical quality to them. Just before the ceremony was about to begin, the rain would stop.

After I announced, "You may seal your vows with a kiss," the couple obliged, the wedding party exited, and the rain would start up again.

As I went to bed that night, I wasn't happy about the prospects of being out in the more than likely bad weather, in the water, and being cold. But then, what did I know for sure? The day could turn out to be absolutely beautiful, and the weather forecaster's inability to accurately tell us what to expect could be affirmed once again.

On the day of the wedding, the scowling weather was nasty and announced a chilly Fall was here. Dark rain clouds ruled out the sunny conditions every wedding couple hopes for. Temperatures dropped fifteen degrees from the high heat of just a few days ago. The night before, the rain was fierce. It drenched the land and created pockets of mud on dirt roads and walkways. I could only guess what the wedding site would look like.

I set out on this adventure right after lunch. Cherie and Frank's location was about an hour's drive away and located in an area I'd never been to before. I'd heard of Fife Lake, and seen the sign pointing to it as I drove by on trips downstate, but I'd never actually been there. As I watched for locator arrows, even a restaurant sign that advertised "Uncle Bob's Barbeque Haven, Fife Lake, Left One Mile" to show me I was on the right track, I'd have been happy. But instead, the signs I remembered from the past had disappeared. Could the lake be the other direction?

Let me be clear. I hate getting lost. This was before GPS was on everyone's phone. All I had to use was the driving directions from Google Maps.com. The satellite that doled out driving instructions must have short-circuited when I typed in their location again on route.

I called Frank on his cell phone, but the "bars" on my phone looked pretty slim. But the phone rang, and it was Cherie. She calmly informed me she didn't really know how to direct me in and called out for help. "Who can tell the minister where she is?"

Carl came on the phone. I was really lost, I explained. He obliged me patiently and assured me he'd help me, just start out, and if you feel lost, call. Thank you, God for sending me a human GPS. At the first nudge of confusion, I called again for guidance down hills, which curves to take to the right, which signs to watch for on the left. I called five times in ten minutes. Or was it six? It's all a blur, just like the morning.

I followed huge electric lines down a rut-carved, sandy road I continued to wait for the latest installment of directions from my guide. Then, from behind me, Frank and Howard showed up in the minivan. Frank looked at me as if finding the ceremony site should have been easy, and said, "Hey. No worries. Follow us."

They pulled ahead of me, and I followed them down a rural road close to where I had first waited for them to come rescue me. Part snake, part sand dune, the road wound itself around young poplars, pines and sumac.

We crawled at five miles per hour in order to navigate around the huge potholes that threatened to break an axle. At last we emerged into a clearing that was staked out by tents and campers. Some twenty people of varying ages, and one very cute, happy pit bull puppy, waited for us.

The air was still quite nippy. The sun was trying to peep out from behind the sky which was full of billowing grey clouds. Wet pines gave off the fragrance of spice and earth. Most of the people gathered for the wedding (except for the puppy) were puffing cigarettes, creating drifts of smoke that floated on the mists of air which forecast what the rest of the ceremony would be like.

I opened the car door and stepped out. Frank looked at me with a crooked smile and said, "You're going to get wet in that." They'd told me to come dressed casually so I wore an old pair of black jeans and a grey shirt that had a few sequins around the neckline.

"You have those waders for me?" I asked.

"Well, this is what I have for you," he said, and pulled out a pair of black beach shoes, the kind that protect a swimmer's feet from the muck and sharp stones on lake bottoms. These were definitely not the "waders" I'd expected, thigh high rubber boots a fisherperson uses when s/he walks into deep water to cast his or her line for trout or bass. "You said size eight, right?"

I nodded yes, getting a bit more nervous about the cold water I had so generously agreed to get into.

"I couldn't find a women's eight. All I could get ya was a man's 6." He held the water shoes out for me to see. "Should work, don't ya think?" He sounded hopeful.

"Well, we'll go with what you've got. It'll be fine," I said, and sat down in the car, the door open, and my legs stretched out so I could put the shoes on.

"You'd better roll your pants up if you want to stay dry. Did you bring a change of clothes?"

"Shoot. No, I didn't," I said aloud. "Well, if I have to, I'll take my jeans off and drive home in my underwear. How fun will that be? I'm not expecting to get out anywhere on my way home. If I get stopped, the cop will hear a good story."

Frank and Howard looked at me like I was half with it, and half out of it. I was used to that kind of look. I'm the kind of person you either think is wonderful or rather nuts.

"Are we ready to go?" I asked.

"Sure, I'll have someone lead you down," Frank said. "If DNR knew I'd made these paths, and built these bridges, we'd probably get kicked out."

The path he led me down was made up of deep green grasses. Ferns and mosses lined the sides. The trees were tall and majestic. I could hear the river the minute I got out of the car. When the path wound around to the bank, the river was about 150 feet wide. Frank mentioned back where the cars were parked the river had swelled from the night's rain. It was running fast, and passed us by like a businessman late for a meeting.

The site became more gorgeous as we walked deeper into the woods. I began to understand why the pristine quality of the place made Cherie and Frank so insistent on having the ceremony here. It was truly peaceful, lovely and sacred as only nature can be.

At one point, a few cement steps had been shimmied into the hill. They were squeezed in between two trees but the incline was uneven and steep. A tall, young man, about twenty-five or so stood at the bottom and reached up to take my hand and help steady my step down. "Thank you," I said, and made a mental note of how considerate Frank had been to put this detail in place.

"We're almost there," Howard assured me.

Further down the path, there were two small lowland meadows that spread out about a foot above where the water appeared to have slowed down. A piece of the shoreline protruded into the river and a little pool of calm water had formed. This made it easier to step down into the river without being shaken by the speed of the rushing water. This was where Frank and I, the best man, maid of honor, brave friends, and eventually, Cherie would enter. A high spot at the edge of the river was designated for the guests to stand to witness the ceremony.

I looked into the clear river. I knew then and there I was glad I had come. Love makes us do lots of things. Even though it wasn't my love, the effect had been the same...I was on an adventure.

I stepped into the water and let the liquid chill wrap itself around me. Because I'd been around water my whole life, I knew if I stayed in it long enough, my body would get used to the frigid temperature. Within a minute, I was acclimated and I hadn't turned blue. This was a good sign.

"How will we know when Cherie is ready?" I asked. Everyone looked at each other as if no one had thought about the cue. Three of the younger men were sent to find the answer, the pit bull puppy following happily after them. A few minutes later they returned and said Cherie was already on her way down.

Frank stood straighter and looked at me to see if I was ready to brave the full force of the flowing water. I wasn't quite ready so I avoided his look. "By the way," I said to him, "you look really nice." He wore a bright white tuxedo shirt opened at the neck. He had on black shorts that also looked like tuxedo pants, but I'd never seen formal shorts before. Another unique detail.

"Thanks," he said. The question of when we should begin our entrance never left his face.

As if on cue, friends started to clap from the ridge above us. I looked up along the craggy fault line, and rising three stories above us, I saw a small cabin. On the undersized porch of the caramel colored log cabin, six people stood holding long, resonant wind chimes. They rang in the clear, distinct tone of church bells, only with a touch of fairy. The music of mystery and reverence floated gently onto those of us below. We were in God's church, built by seed, sand and stone.

The silence was punctuated by a few shouts from the shoreline by this group of resourceful people who'd made the best of what they'd been given. Out of their regard for Frank and Cherie, here they were, standing out in this nasty weather, and this far away from civilization to be with their friends who were getting married. My spirit felt joyful. For Cherie and Frank, I couldn't help but feel grateful.

Frank stepped into the swift water. "Yeah, we might as well go," I said. Frank smiled, and offered me his hand. Again, I let myself accept this act of kindness. We turned towards the area Frank told me was shallowest, and perfect for the ceremony. What I didn't hear was that if I didn't follow him exactly, in no time at all, I'd get really wet.

Yes, I got really wet. The water swirled up to my crotch.

I must've taken a deep breath, because Frank turned and looked back at me. I swear he wanted to laugh, but didn't. "Follow that ridge in the water," he instructed and pointed to the place he'd just left behind.

What ridge? I couldn't see anything. What was I looking for? At this point, it didn't matter. I was wet. Wet to the bone. And not minding it a bit. Actually, I was quite delighted. I'm doing a wedding in a river, I thought. How cool is this?!!!

My feet sloshed in my too big beach shoes as I toddled after Frank who continued to move forward. His best man, my directions savior, Carl, followed behind me. The riverbed rose and showed the sand bar ahead. Frank pointed out this was where he and his friends would bring their lawn chairs and brews when it was hot and just sit in the middle of the spitting river to relax. The wind that was blowing through the trees carried the sharp smell of burning tobacco away from us. I paid attention instead to the beauty that nature offered through the air, the land, the water, the trees and foliage.

Someone from above began to strum a guitar and the notes drifted down like soft rose petals. From their vantage point the wedding guests could see Cherie before either Frank or I could. When she appeared, I saw the star tattoo peeking out from under her short, creamy white, flowing wedding dress. She had flowers in her hair. She looked lovely and carried herself with dignity.

Cherie was the perfect example of a natural woman. She and her bridesmaid waded out to the shallows, the hem of her dress barely touching the river water. I was sure fairies were attending her, holding the water away from reaching up to weigh down her gown. She didn't smile, but walked toward us matter-of-factly, elegant in her simplicity. The river seemed to respect her as the sun tried to come out again, and a few sparkles on the water reflected into her face.

Next to her was her Maid of Honor, Amanda. She had a sweet, round face, and glistening straight black hair that scattered as it cascaded down her back. Both women carried bouquets of daisies, wildflowers, clover and pine fronds.

As Cherie got closer, I smiled and prompted Amanda to take Cherie's flowers so Cherie could hold Frank's hands. She noticed I was curious about the simple ribbon bound flower arrangement. As she handed the bouquet to Amanda, she said to me, "I gathered them on my way down." She turned to face Frank. They smiled at each other and their eyes met. She looked down shyly at first, then raised her head and looked straight into his eyes which had never left her face.

I knew by the loud sound of the river that the thirty feet the people on the river side wouldn't hear a thing I said unless I shouted. So, I said to Frank and Cherie, "Excuse me for a minute," and sloshed a few feet sideways, facing their guests.

"Now I know all you people came here to watch Frank and Cherie get married," I shouted. "But if you want to hear anything, you're gonna have to get brave like the rest of us in this river and come on in." The water rushing by was the only sound. "Are you all chicken?" I asked when no one moved. "Then just cheer when you see them kiss," I yelled.

This effort to get folks to participate put big smiles on Frank and Cherie's faces. Frank waved to their friends. I asked them, "Are you ready," and when they nodded, I began.

"We've been brought together today to witness and celebrate an act of deep commitment and love. Cherie and Frank, in your devotion, respect, and love for each other is it true that you wish to unite in the holy bond of marriage, and to dedicate yourselves to each other's happiness and well-being as life mates, partners and lovers of the planet?"

"Yes, we do," they answered.

I acknowledged the role their friends played in helping Frank and Cherie find each other and made one more attempt to get their friends involved in the ceremony. I shouted, "Although this is their day, it is also a tribute to all of you. For knowing you and interacting with you has helped to make Cherie and Frank who they needed to be to find each other. Each one of you is an important piece in the story of their life. You all hold a place in their hearts reserved for those that they have chosen to call 'Family' and 'Friends' and they're deeply grateful for each and every one of you here today."

I reminded Frank and Cherie that they had known each other for eleven years, and felt a connection with each other from the beginning. "Ten years ago, Cherie came to a Labor Day party that Frank was at, which led to you two being friends. After all this time of being great companions, both honoring our beautiful planet, you 'get' each other. Cherie, you are spontaneous, and Frank, you're the organized one…great complements to each other. You just need a porch, two rocking chairs, and that's about all you have to have to start talking about anything and everything. It's an added plus that Frank laughs at your jokes, isn't it, Cherie?" She didn't respond, just kept looking into his eyes.

At this point, it started to sprinkle, and the sky got darker. In the interests of beating mother nature to the punch, I cut out a fair portion of the ceremony and moved to their vows. First, they gave each other their rings, simple bands that had the light weight of tungsten. Frank began, "With this ring, I pledge to you my heart, and my faithfulness forever. I take you as my wife." Cherie repeated the same words and placed Frank's ring finger on his left hand.

Instead of speaking traditional vows, they'd asked to do the Celtic Hand-fasting Ceremony. For this ceremony, they used six ribbons. I read a statement that they appropriately agreed or disagreed with, and then, I draped one of the cords over their joined hands, saying, "And so the binding is made." Cherie had weighted the ribbons with beads at both ends which helped to keep the ribbons from blowing off in the wind.

The ceremony continued as a stiff wind blew along the river into our shallows. The water rippled from the drafts of air. Amanda held the ribbons, and his best man stood next to me and held the wedding script. I began:

"Now that your lives have crossed, you have formed ties between each other. The promises you make today and the ties that are bound here will cross the years and greatly strengthen your union. With full awareness, know that you declare your intent to be hand-fasted before your friends and families. Do you seek to enter this ceremony?"

"Yes, we seek to enter."

"I bid you to look into one another's eyes."

The ceremony continued as I asked the questions that led to draping one cord around their hands. One after the other, I asked, and they answered until the final cord laid over their hands. The knots of this binding are not formed by these cords, but rather by your vows. For always, you hold in your own hands the making or breaking of this union.

The moment was sweet, but suddenly I felt the bite of the chilled air, my feet freezing cold underwater. The wind was whipping in the trees, and the breeze flipped the pages of the ceremony over in my brown leather binder. I offered the traditional Irish Blessing and with blue sky above being for another day, the ceremony was over. I invited them to "Seal your vows with a smooch."

The kiss came, and the heavens were filled with a chorus of deep chimes. Whomever had been playing music had brought out what looked like multiple sets of wind chimes. The magic of having the music of the Bells of Westminster in the woods, ringing strong and true lasted about 30 seconds. One of their friends, NOT full of charm and grace, startled everyone into a crouching position when he set off three booming firecracker blasts. The sound was so loud that the riverbed under my feet twitched. The water shimmied as if it was in a glass being shaken against ice cubes. Even Frank was surprised, and yelled out, "Geesh, what the…" and glanced back at me as if my being a minister was the stopper needed to cork the bottle before it exploded with expletives. But Cherie, unflappable, calm, took his hand and turned to wave at their friends like nothing had happened. She was focused on the chimes, and the drops of rain that had started to fall.

Frank nodded to Carl and his best man offered his arm to me as we formed the recessional. Amanda linked arms with a younger girl I assumed was her daughter, and brought up the rear. The chimes sang, "they are one, they are one" in my imagination. This is magic, I thought.

Smoke from the firecrackers drifted across the river like a thick streamer, then was scooped up by the wind and disappeared into the slight fog. A new, low grey cloud sneered down at us, telepathically hurrying us along with its deep and low rumbling threats. If we took too long, we'd soon be sopping wet from head to toe instead of waist to toe.

But Cherie was not in the mood to hurry. This was a day she'd remember for the rest of her life. She was going to take it all in, the brisk air, friends standing like toys on the shore, the deep, long ringing of the chimes, the rain drops weighing the grasses down. Frank relaxed and adjusted to her pace, seeing what she was seeing.

I, on the other hand, stumbled and wobbled on river rocks. You'd have thought I was determined to help the river swallow me whole. Carl, tuned into the river's sanguine nature, did his best to navigate the way. But the weather was getting a little too rowdy for me. I tried to pick up the pace despite Cherie's right to enjoy every moment.

Although I never fell in the water, I should have. I was fairly wet from the top of my jeans on down at this point. I valued the parts of my body that were still dry enough to be willing to risk completely falling into the water by pushing faster through it. I tried to outpace the chilly rain I could feel beginning to come down. But for every couple of steps forward, I faltered for three. When I reached the shore, I looked back at Cherie and Frank who were arm in arm, smiling, still waving at the chime ringers, calling out to their friends who were waving beer bottles in celebration.

As I regained my footing on the soggy ground, I realized that I had just shared very intimate moments with this couple, and had a mist-ical adventure!

I fell in line with the few others who were also walking quickly up the path back to the base camp. Some people had remained near their tents rather than witness the ceremony, but I guessed the firecracker's boom signaled it was time to pack up and head back to another site for the celebration and food. Rain started to come down and once I reached where the cars were parked, the campfires were spitting back at the insistent drops that were trying to douse them.

I opened the car door and grabbed a thick grey towel I kept in the back seat, and laid it on the seat. I sloshed my wet rear end onto the seat. My pants felt more like ice cube funnels, and when they touched my legs, sent a shiver up my spine.

"Yowser," I exclaimed, and rolled the pants up as far as I could to keep them off my skin. The keys to the car were buried in the deep pockets of my raincoat, but when I pulled them out and twisted the key in the starter, the red car fired right up. I pulled the door shut and turned on the heat. The rain started to run in rivulets down the windshield.

Three "gets" had yet to happen: 1. Get the license signed by the witnesses. 2. Get Frank and Cherie to sign the marriage license. 3. Get paid.

I pulled out the written copy of the ceremony I'd give them and their marriage license. In the rearview mirror, I saw Frank walk up to the car, and he looked concerned. "Are you okay?" he asked.

Quite cheerfully I said, "Oh sure." Then I laughed saying, "Lovely day, eh?" I must've had a "you owe me money" tone of voice because he did a little jump and said, "Oh, geez, let me get you your check."

"I need the witnesses to sign, Frank. Can you get them to come sign in the car?"

Frank yelled out to Carl and Amanda to "get their butts over here to sign the license." They sprinted to the car and crawled into the back seat to dutifully sign. Cherie floated over when Frank called her, slowly and neatly signed her new name. Then she gave me a hug. "Thank you for being so accommodating," she said. "Everything you said was perfect."

I started to purr. "I'm glad I could be part of this today. It was really fun. Thank you for asking me."

Frank reached in and handed me the check which I accepted with a thank you. "Frank, I need you to sign now," I ordered. "Come sit inside."

"No, no, I will sign in my car. I'll keep it dry. Don't wanna get your car wetter." He smiled his toothy, warm smile. I handed him the license, which I tucked safely inside of a big white envelope. He took it, got into his minivan, signed both copies, and handed them back.

Last but not least I signed, and explained what was in the envelope and what they had to do in order for Cherie to change her name on all legal documents.

"Can you find your way back out onto the road?" Frank asked me.

"I have your number if I get lost."

"Hey, I'll lead her out," Carl said.

"You are a true gentleman," I told him, and rearranged my pants that were warming up and losing their stiffness. The rain had slowed down. The puppy and half the people had already left.

Cherie and Frank stood outside the car and looked in on me. "This has been quite a great experience for me, you two. I know you will be very happy." Frank pulled Cherie closer and gave her a kiss on the cheek. She smiled softly at him, and at me. I knew they would never be the kind of people who would put on airs or pretend they were anyone other than who they were. "You know, this river is a great symbol for the power of love that will run through your life together. I think that's pretty cool."

They laughed, and waved good-bye. I put the car in reverse, followed Carl for the next winding mile, and headed home.

When I stopped for gas I considered taking my soggy pants off, but decided to keep them on as a badge of honor. I didn't want to break the spell of the ringing of the chimes and being immersed in nature. Frank and Cherie gave me so many gifts of aliveness. I was grateful to have had the privilege of marrying people who loved each other, and to step with them into the magical waters of life.

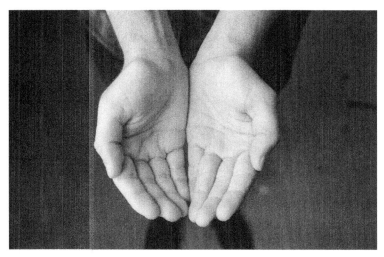

Photo by Andrew Moca on Unsplash.com

21 HANDS

This ceremony is definitely one of the most popular reading/special ceremonies. Couple's love it because they really don't have to do anything (unless they are game to try the Bit of Dazzle) and the last line usually touches people hearts. I use it 95% of the time near the end of their full ceremony.

I always advise my couple that while this is a wonderful ceremony, "By the time you've gotten this far you're going to want to kiss each other. You'll probably be looking into each other's eyes instead of at your hands like you're supposed to. Do your best to listen to what I'm saying, and keep your eyes on your hands if you can." Maybe they can, and maybe they can't. The last sentence usually gets a response from the guests because it's so touching. This makes the ceremony as much for those attending as it is for the couple.

NOTE: Check to make sure the couple wants to have children. If not, delete line seven. The unknown author won't mind.

Script

[Couple's Names], please take each other's hands, palms up so you may see the gift that they are to you:

These are the hands of your best friend, young and strong and vibrant with love, that are holding yours on your wedding day, as you promise to love one another all the days of your life.

These are the hands that will work alongside yours as together you build your future.

These are the hands that will passionately love you and cherish you through the years, and with the slightest touch will comfort you like no other.

These are the hands that will hold you when fear or grief temporarily comes your way.

These are the hands that will countless times wipe the tears from your eyes, tears of sorrow and tears of joy. These are the hands that will tenderly hold your children.

These are the hands that will give you support and encouragement to chase down your dreams.

These are the hands that will hold you tight as you struggle through difficult times.

These are the hands that will give you strength when you need it.

These are the hands that will lift your chin and brush your cheek as they raise your face to look into eyes that are filled with overwhelming love for you.

And lastly, these are the hands that even when wrinkled and aged will still be reaching for yours, still giving you the same unspoken tenderness with just a touch.

A Bit of Dazzle

When you have a couple is into acting, they can make hand gestures, such as the part, "wipe the tears from your eyes," they actually act out wiping tears from each other's eyes. Or "Lift your chin and brush your cheek" they can touch each other's cheek or lift their chin to look into each other's eyes.

22 HAWAIIAN STYLE WEDDING TRADITIONS

The Revs. Ken and Judy Grimes lived on Maui for 10+ years and did thousands of weddings because wedding season there continues all year around. During our conversations, they told me about common elements in traditional Hawaiian wedding ceremonies and how their special brand of ceremony could be changed to include them. As a resource provider to your couples, any one of these traditions can give your warm weather-loving couples a fun edge. If your couple is interested in adding these elements, you might even talk them into creating a large area of sand so you can lead the ceremony Hawaiian style!

Overview
A conch shell is usually sounded at the beginning of a ceremony to signify its start. Finding someone who can blow into and get a sound from a conch shell is the quest.

Encourage any wedding planners to decorate the altar area and aisle chairs with palm fronds, shells hanging on ribbons, conch shells around the tropical silk flower arrangements.

When you think of a wedding song and Hawaii, The Hawaiian Wedding Song, written in 1926, and sung by Elvis Presley in 1961, would most likely come to mind. Another song that comes to mind and so is often played at weddings in Hawaii is Somewhere Over the Rainbow (1939) sung by Israel "IZ" Kamakawiwo'ole recorded in 2010.

Resource
Online source for leis: Shaka Leis. See Link Directory

Wedding Dress

Partner1 – a Pikake lei which is long and made up of little white flowers in the jasmine family. Partner 1 can also wear a Haku lei or flower headpiece. Partner2 – a Maile lei with white orchid or tuberose, and is much longer than the one worn by Partner1.

Partner1's maids – white spiral orchid lei

Partner2's groomsmen – Ti Leaf Maile lei

Early in the ceremony, when the couple comes to the officiant, they can be handed their lei by an attendant, or a respected family member or friend.

Sometimes the officiant drapes the Maile lei around the couple's necks. But it's always someone else who puts the lei around your neck. Do not put the lei around your own neck--no, no, no!!

The couple may wear matching shirts or a muumuu that matches the other Partner's shirt.

Script

Your choice.

Conclusion

After the ceremony is completed, a photo is always taken inside the outline of a heart drawn in the sand. If the couple is in Maui or wants to pretend they're in Maui, then etch into the sand "Just Mauied".

Optional: Occasionally we may be hired to officiate for a couple who then decides to make their ceremony into a destination wedding. If they go to Hawaii, you can give them some ideas to take with them, and be a help to them in this way.

A Bit of Dazzle

Here's a blessing to add: May the beauty that you feel in your hearts for one another and symbolized by your leis shower you with more love, more joy, and many peaceful walks along the beach/road of life together.

23 HERB

This ceremony is an easy modification of the Sand Ceremony but with a different kind of symbolism. Usually a glass jar is used to hold the herbs, but there's a more substantial feel if a pottery container is used instead. Some vessels because they're more porous, may absorb some of the herbs' fragrances. This gives the added symbolism of how the power of the herb/their love is a delight to all their senses for a long time to come.

Supplies Needed
A pint or quart-sized vessel
Loose-leaf amounts of herbs and spices you choose
OR
Each herb or spice in its own content-identified pouch

Officiant: [Couple's Names], your marriage not only joins you together as a couple, it also joins your two families together in meaningful, and supportive relationships. In this bond, each of you brings your own unique energy, so who you are contributes to the whole of your family and friends. In fact, each of you adds to the spice of life.

As you to your lives as a married couple, you blend together your strengths that will balance and augment any weaknesses of your partner. As your family and friends are brought together, the energy of their presence also contributes to the uniqueness of the whole.

[Couple's Names], the spirit of life has given you the ability to choose the energies you will share with one another. You've chosen the herbs (name of herb or spice) and (name of herb or spice) which represent (see below) and (see below).

NOTE: Name as many herbs as there are people.

To represent your family and friends, you've chosen) the herbs _____ (and _____) which represent _____ (and _____). As you blend these leaves and seeds together, it symbolizes how your energy is uniquely blended to produce the sweet variety of life.

Officiant: Everyone here wishes for you to remember your uniqueness, and the delightful mixture you've made to help and encourage each other on your way in life. May it make you stronger, and be a reminder of the joy of this day.

Couple return to their place with the officiant.

Photo by Visual Stories || Micheile on Unsplash.com

Herbs and Their Energetic Properties

Alfalfa – prosperity Bay – protection, strength
Chamomile – money, love, purification, peace
Frankincense – spirituality
Heather – luck
Jasmine – Love, money, prophetic dreams
Lavender – love, protection, happiness, peace
Lemon Balm – love, healing
Licorice root -- fidelity
Marigold – legal matters, prophecy
Mugwort – psychic awareness, strength
Myrrh – protection, spirituality
Peppermint – healing, psychic powers, purification
Pennyroyal – protection, courage, strength, harmony
Rose – love, luck, divination
Rosemary – purification, mental health
Sage – wisdom, longevity

A Bit of Dazzle

If the couple are cooks, they can choose herbs and spices to make a special combination they can prepare or set out because of the fragrance. Create a recipe, cook the dish and pass the recipe out to guests.

Another option is if they're creating a combination of herbs and spices they plan to use, go big! They'll need a very large jar or mixing bowl, and in the ceremony, combine a large quantity of their herbs or spices, and during the reception, divide the concoction up into pouches to give as gifts to their guests. If this option sounds fun, someone must be delegated to do the packaging and distributing to the guests.

HOLIDAY CEREMONIES

24 NEW YEARS

This ceremony can also be interactive. Keeping the commitment they're making to each other central, and yet promoting how this is a new and fresh start for them makes this ceremony a fun adaptation of a common ceremony.

Script

Officiant: Throughout the memory of humanity, a time has been set aside to celebrate letting go of the past year and its obligations, and celebrating the arrival of a fresh, new day. We all need new beginnings and a time to let our guard down and celebrate, celebrate, celebrate!

How appropriate is it, that on New Year's Eve, when we take the time to make resolutions, plans, and aspirations for the year ahead that we're here with [Couple's Names] to celebrate the beginning of their life together as a married couple.

This is a brand-new beginning for them where celebrating their love and commitment to each other seems to naturally have its own sparkle. But the vows they make to one another is no less monumental and important because of the atmosphere of readiness, freshness, and happiness.

New Year's Eve's ceremony tonight is a happy dance into the mystery of [Couple's Names] future.

Together we'll send them forward with all the love and support we can offer. But also, we wish for them that on this eve of a new year, they let go of what no longer serves them from the past, so they may, with open hands and open hearts, fully welcome each other as life mates and partners, making a new fresh start together.

[Couple's Names] are so grateful you're here with them today. And they also hope this ceremony gives each of you a chance to step into your own fresh beginning on their wedding day.

Wedding Address

We're here together to claim with them the good that comes from their shared past and to envision the brightest and best of futures, where they continue to discover the path into a new beginning as a married couple.

We're sharing with them the passage from one year into the next, from living a solitary life to living a life where two become one.

Neither state, church, family relations nor tradition alone, enact a ceremony or further the expectation that the true joining of two people begins on a certain date, no matter how significant that date may be. Such unity comes only through love freely given.

[Couple's Names], it's in your power and your power alone to let the past go and be ready, truly ready to celebrate your love in the new year.

By your joy, the sincerity of your purpose, the strength of your common devotion, and the enduring character of your dedication, are you ready to leave one year behind and celebrate your love in the new year to come?

Answer: Yes!

Statements of Intention

Partner2, do you ask Partner1 to be your wife/husband and promise before God and this company that you will love her/him, honor her/him and comfort her/him whether your life experience is filled with abundance or lack, health or sickness, joy or sorrow, being loyal to her/him as long as you both shall live?

Answer: Yes.

And, Partner1, do you grant Partner2's request to be his/her wife/husband?

Answer: I do. Repeat for Partner1.

Affirmation by Family and Guests

Do you, family and guests promise [Couple's Names] your love and encouragement in their new life together, from this moment on? If so please answer together, "We will." ANSWER: "We will."

Wedding Address continued

Jane Wells wrote in 1886, "Let your love be stronger than your hate or anger. Learn the wisdom of compromise, for it is better to bend a little than to break. Believe the best rather than the worst. People have a way of living up or down to your opinion of them. Remember that true friendship is the basis for any lasting relationship. The person you choose to marry is deserving of the courtesies and kindnesses you bestow on your friends.

Optional: Please hand this down to your children and your children's children."

Partner1 and Partner2, this advice is just as true today as it was over one hundred years ago. Your marriage must stand, neither by the authority of the state nor by the words of the Officiant, but by the strength of your love and the power of faith in each other and in the Divine Love that has opened up the way into your new year and all the years ahead of you as a married couple. It is nurtured by your awe of the power and beauty of nature.

It should never be said of either of you that you show more concern for a friend than you do for each other. More kindness, gentleness, and concern needs to be shown in the privacy of your own home than anywhere else. Your home is a haven from all the confusion and craziness the world can create. And faithfulness to each other every day is the primary ingredient that will produce the joy that you seek.

Exchange of Rings
May I have the rings please as a token of devotion to your beloved?

Notice that these rings are a circle without beginning nor end. They are made of precious metal to represent the precious nature of your relationship. Whenever you look at these rings, may you recall this day and the love you have promised.

Partner2, please put this ring on Partner1's finger and repeat after me:

I give you this ring as symbol of my love and commitment.

Partner1, please put this ring on Partner2's finger and repeat after me:

I give you this ring as symbol of my love and commitment.

Blessing of the Rings
Bless these rings, Creator of all living beings, of the sun, the moon, the earth, the skies, the water. May the giver and the receiver grow in the richness of Your Love, living together in growing appreciation and respect

for each other and their relationship as the years unfold. May they dance in celebration of the wonder of Love as it lives in and through them. Amen.

Pronouncement and Kiss
Now that you have proclaimed your vows and exchanged rings, please seal your commitment with a kiss.

Introduction of the New Year's Couple
May I introduce to you newlyweds, [Couple's First and Last Names]!

Happy New Year everyone!

A Bit of Dazzle
If there's an archway, you can signify that as they stand on their current side of the archway, they're standing in the past year, and when they walk through the archway, they are walking into the new year together to start fresh and new.

Option: Before you pronounce the couple married, have guests stand and state their New Year's best wishes or resolutions for the couple.

OR -- Have people write on a piece of rice paper their New Year's wish or resolution for the couple before they enter for the ceremony. Place in a jar. Choose a few of the wishes and read them aloud to the couple.

25 VALENTINES DAY

Background

St. Valentine's Day, as we know it today, contains vestiges of both Christian and ancient Roman tradition.

One legend contends that Valentine was a priest who served during the third century in Rome. When Emperor Claudius II decided that single men made better soldiers than those with wives and families, he outlawed marriage for young men. Valentine, realizing the injustice of the decree, defied Claudius and continued to perform marriages for young lovers in secret. When Valentine's actions were discovered, Claudius ordered that he be put to death.

According to another legend, an imprisoned Valentine actually sent the first "valentine" greeting himself after he fell in love with a young girl—possibly his jailor's daughter—who visited him during his confinement. Before his death, it is alleged that he wrote her a letter signed "From your Valentine," an expression that is still in use today. Although the truth behind the Valentine legends is unconfirmed, the stories all emphasize his appeal as a sympathetic, heroic and—most importantly—romantic figure.

This ceremony is short and sweet. Decorations are prime on Valentine's Day so we'll let the pinks, the roses and chocolates do most of the talking.

Process

Prior to the ceremony ask the couple what brought you together? You may want to prompt them, for example, "Was it a tasty meal? A sports event or at a movie?" Their answers will be incorporated below.

"Love must be as much a light as it is a flame."
Henry David Thoreau, author and poet

Script

Officiant: We're here on this winter's day because [Couple's Names] know how easy it is to forget their anniversary date, and wanted something easy to remember. Of course, they want the flame to get brighter, and the light to shine farther because they are together.

But they also want to get married today because it's as if the whole world is celebrating with them.

And this will happen year after year after year!

[Couple's Names], think back to the day you first met, to the time the sparks first flew, and then to the day one of you proposed and the other said "Yes!"

What brought you together? This is the romance that began your growth as a couple. It is just a beginning. *(Incorporate ideas shared with you during your interview.)*

Because although Valentine's Day is special, its most important reminder is in this quote by an anonymous source:

> *"Love is a verb. It's an action thing and it's what you do that matters. It's not what we say, it's what we do to demonstrate the love."*

May you do right by each other, expect the best from each other, and bring out the soulful, generous and loving side of each other, day after day, year after year.

Are you ready to share your vows?

Answer: Yes!

Vows

Partner1 to Partner2: I, [Partner1's Name], vow to you, [Partner2's Name], to be the man/woman you inspire me to be and I vow to be the husband/wife you deserve. I promise to share my heart openly with you and to build a future that is nurturing, supportive, and a celebration of all that's good and bold and beautiful within us. I will love you forever and a day.

Repeat for Partner2.

Exchange of Rings

Because I love you with all my heart. I give you this ring as a pledge to you my loyalty, respect, and passion for as long as we both live.

Rings are exchanged.

Blessing

Thank you, God for all the beauty in the world, for its promise and fulfillment. For chocolate and roses, wine and cheese, good jokes and bad jokes but always laughter. We appreciate the power of love between [Couple's Names] and affirm that year after year, their love will grow until their hearts are overflowing with happiness and joy. May their passion for one another live forever. Amen

Pronouncement

In honor of the Love that wants to become more in and through you and by the power vested in me by the State of _____, I now passionately pronounce you married!

A Bit of Dazzle

As a part of exchanging their vows, have the couple exchange a rose, take a bite out of a Valentine's Day chocolate, and sip from the same glass of wine.

26 FOURTH OF JULY

A wedding is a celebration of the union of two free people. Because Independence Day is about our freedom as a country, and a celebration of our choice to be united together as its citizens, the couple who choose this date for their wedding ceremony may have an extra devotion to the principles of liberty and justice for all.

This ceremony also has an opportunity to be interactive. It invites guests to share a story about love or the couple.

Caution: Don't overdo the red, white and blue theme!

Script

Officiant: Today is a celebration of the union of two free people. A celebration of how the sparks fly between [Couple's Names] because of their love, commitment, and friendship. They're two people who are in it forever.

Not all ceremonies emphasize a couple's freedom to choose. But here they are, standing on a stage, looking patriotic surrounded by the red, white and blue decorations, and being gazed at by pretty much everyone who has meant something to them.

They know how important liberty and freedom are to love. Despite any differences, love is what we all share. It's the great unifier — our one universal truth. No matter who we are, where we've come from, what we believe, we know this one thing: love is what we're doing right.

That's why [Couple's Names] are both are standing here. That's why everyone is here to witness this ceremony. We have all loved in our lifetimes, and may even have felt the pain of the loss of freedom. But in this moment, we're reminded that the ability to love is the very best part of our humanity and is at the core of our celebration of life that overcomes any unhealthy bonds that may try to inhibit us.

Every one of us who are here today has their own love stories. Just as we have our own definitions of freedom. Some are short; others long. Some are yet unwritten, while others are just getting to the good part. There are chapters in all of our stories that are sad or disappointing — and others that are exciting and full of adventure.

Insert an anecdote from the couple's love story here.

And that brings [Couple's Names] here. A time to pause, look back, and smile at all the moments that brought them here. A time to imagine what moments are still to come. To share in their unique freedom of expression and opinion.

We're all here because we want those moments for you, [Couple's Names]. We're here to hope with you, to support you, to be proud of you, and to remind you that love isn't necessarily happily ever after. Love is the experience of freedom that comes with making a commitment to love. It's about writing your story of love.

It's not one moment — not even this moment. It's every moment. Big ones like saying "I love you," *(Add your own examples such as "moving in together, getting engaged, making dinner together, spending holidays with your families, binge-watching TV shows, getting a big hug when you get home from work".)*

These everyday moments fuse together into one big experience that continuously expands how we experience freedom, and have the liberty to love as we choose. So today, we have some words about what love is, coming from some of the people who love you the most.

Insert readings or a few select personal stories told by friends or family members.

Officiant: You fell in love by chance, but you're here today because you're making a choice. You both are choosing each other. You've chosen to be with someone who enhances you, who makes you think, makes you smile, and makes every day brighter.

You're about to make promises to each other that you intend to keep. You're going to vow to take care of each other, to stand up for one another, and find happiness with each other. There's a simple premise to each of these promises: you're vowing to be there. You're teaming up and saying to the other, "Every experience I have, I want you to be a part of everything I do."

Consent and Vows

Will you, [Partner1], keep [Partner2] as your favorite person — to laugh with her/him, go on adventures with her/him, support her/him through life's tough moments, be proud of her/him, grow old with her/him, and find new reasons to love her/him every day?

Partner1: I will. [Repeat for Partner2]

Partner2: I will.

Officiant: Will you, [Couple's Names] be each other's partners from this day forward? Will you bring out the best in one another, share your happiest moments together, and love each other freely and absolutely — for the rest of this lifetime?

Partners1 and 2: We will.

Officiant: Please feel free to share your personal vows with each other now.

Exchange of Rings

Officiant: You've both chosen to wear rings as a reminder of these vows. People often say wedding bands are a perfect circle, with no beginning and no end. But these rings did have a beginning. The stones were formed a long time ago deep with the earth. Eventually, a series of lucky events caused them to rise to the surface, where someone dug them up. Metal was then liquefied in a furnace at a thousand degrees—molded, cooled, and painstakingly polished. Something beautiful was made from raw elements.

Love is like that. It comes from humble beginnings, and through a combination of serendipity and effort, imperfect beings shape it into something extraordinary. It's the process of making something beautiful where there was once nothing at all. As you look at these rings over the years, I hope you remember you've created something invaluable. I know you'll protect these rings, and the freedoms and commitments you've made to one another today.

Closing

[Toast adapted from Blessing for a Marriage by James Dillett Freeman]

May your marriage bring you all the exquisite excitements a marriage should bring.

May you need one another, but not out of weakness.

May you want one another, but not out of lack.

May you look for things to praise, often say, "I love you!" and take no notice of small faults.

May you have happiness, and may you find it making one another happy. May you have love, and may you find it loving one another.

Pronouncement

Under the authority of the laws of the land and in honor of your freedom to love and live and pursue happiness together, I now pronounce you married! And KISS to seal your vows. I happily introduce to you as [Preferred Introduction].

A Bit of Dazzle

Before the couple shares their vows, drape the American flag around their shoulders as in the Navajo Wedding Blanket ceremony or the Lasso Ceremony. If the couple really wants to go overboard on the 4th of July them of freedom, Thomas Jefferson wrote the following on June 24, 1826

> *"May it [the Declaration of Independence] be to the world, what I believe it will be, the signal of arousing [all people] to burst the chains…and to assume the blessings and security of self-government. That form, which we have substituted, restore the free right to the unbounded exercise of reason and freedom of opinion. All eyes are opened, or opening to the rights of all. For ourselves, let the annual return of this day forever refresh our recollections of these rights, and an undiminished devotion to them."*

27 HALLOWEEN

There are lots of people who are in love with Halloween. Not all Officiants are open to doing this kind of a ceremony. But if you are, it's important to keep a sense of reverence when the couple exchanges their vows.

Script
Welcome and Opening Words
On behalf of every skull and cross-bone, ghost and vampire, and every witch and warlock who has been enchanted by you and holds you near to their haunted house, thank you [Couple's Names], for choosing each other. You two are part of the hallowed, and yes, holy, showing how it can surprise and delight you no matter what the circumstances are.

Your experiences through the highs and lows, ups and downs of discovering what love is has brought you here today. You have your hopes and dreams of what love can be and how you can dance through eternity together. You are walking together into the mystery of what love has yet to show you about the wonder of who you are as lovers and tricksters, with the power of two acting as one.

You're brave; you are amazing. You are in for quite an adventure!

You will always be discovering heart-pounding magic and wonder in each other. We can assure you -- you'll fall in love many times but always with the eerie newness you uncover in each other. You've already been finding out what your common screams and curses are, and both bring you together creating a spine-tingling union that's led you to make this important commitment to each other today.

Do you acknowledge that in each other, you've found your matching apparition and best friend? A deeply charmed and satisfying marriage must have the bond of enchanted friendship as its foundation for in friendship, there are realistic expectations; the psychic knowledge of another as you finish each other's sentences, and the willingness to speak in tongues of love. You need to have someone you can depend on who will speak truthfully with you, and, will not resort to anger, blame or shame to get what you want but instead cast spells and perform good magic. Respect each for your ability to enchant above all else.

The following reading talks about your love, and that it will never die.

Reading – Lumps of Clay
You and I have so much love,
    That it burns like a fire,
    In which we bake a lump of clay
    Molded into a figure of you
    And a figure of me.
    Then we take both of them.
    And break them into pieces,
    And mix the pieces with water,
    And mold again a figure of you
    And a figure of me.
    I am in your clay.
    You are in my clay.
    Optional: In life we share a single quilt,
    In death we will share one coffin.

Statements of Intention

[Couple's Name], have you come here freely and without reservation to give yourselves to each other in marriage?

Response: Yes.

Consent

Do you, [Partner2] take [Partner1] as your spouse, being faithful to her/him, tenderly loving her/him, honoring her/him, and offering encouragement and companionship through all the magic that may come in your life together?

Response: I do.

Repeat for the other partner.

Exchange of Rings

Please take your rings out, and close your bones and fingers around them.

These rings you're exchanging today are a powerful symbol of resilience, the undeniable strength you have to make it through whatever zombies and monsters may come. Your rings are circles which means they're symbolic of the power of the moon and of the revolving, evolving inner earth. Your rings repeat constantly that the Love which created the light and the darkness has no beginning and no end. The jewels represent the haunting beauty of your hallowed love.

Vows

Officiant: [Partner 2], please repeat after me: [Partner1], I take you as my deeply treasured wife/husband. Neither darkness nor eye of newt can take away the love I have for you. From this day to the grave, I dedicate every bone in my body to showering you with love and affection. I am yours forever body, mind and soul.

The wedding ring is placed on Partner1's finger and s/he repeats: I give you this ring…as a symbol…of my undying…hallowing love and commitment.

Repeat for the other partner.

Halloween Zen

Take note of the chill in the air and howling sounds of the werewolves, mummies and zombies.

Feel all around you at what it's like to be here, surrounded by the shadows of those who traveled near and far to be with you, because they love you and wish only the best hauntings for both of you, forever.

Drink in the sight, sound and feel of the person standing here with you whom you love more than anyone else.

Notice the feeling of each other's hands, and the weight of the rings on your boney fingers.

Lastly, remember back to the very first moment you met. Back when this Halloween love started, and how that fateful night transported you here today.

Pronouncement and Kiss

[Couple's Names], by proclaiming your undying love and commitment to each other in the presence of this company of witches and warlocks (may substitute friends and loved ones), you have joined your bleeding hearts as one. In the spirit of all beginnings, which has brought you together in marriage, I now pronounce you wonderfully, marvelously married.

You may seal your vows with a bite.

A Bit of Dazzle

Seriously, you want more? Okay, then dress up as a witch or warlock with multi-colored hair. Practice a cackle and after the couple is introduced to guests, the Officiant lets out a big cackle laugh.

28 THANKSGIVING

This ceremony acknowledges the similarities between gratitude, thankfulness and appreciation. Because this ceremony may be based around a meal it is short and sweet. The ceremony has a touch of interactivity, so put on your cheerleader's cap!

Script

Welcome family and friends. Today is a welcome addition to the traditional way we celebrate Thanksgiving. Thank you for coming from near and far to share this day with [Couple's Names]. They know it's a big change to rearrange your traditional celebration to attend their wedding. They are very grateful, and promise you, we are all going to have such a great time!

Officiant to everyone: Are you thankful to be here together for this wonderful occasion? If so say together "We are thankful!"

Today is about the big picture. It's not just a celebration of the incredible mix of people who make up our great country, it's a celebration of [Couple's Names] love, but also how the power of gratitude can change a challenge into a blessing.

It's about generosity, and good fortune. It's to see the power of thankfulness among friends, family, and even a few strangers. It's the ultimate expression of gratitude for the people who have supported all of us and especially [Couple's Names] beginning their life together as a married couple.

To be thankful is to appreciate. Appreciation is defined as a feeling or expression of admiration, approval, or gratitude. For example, when Partner2 says to Partner1, "I want to express my appreciation for all you've done to make me a better person." It joins their hearts together even more.

A strong marriage also nurtures [Couple's Names] as separate individuals and allows them both to maintain their unique identity and grow in their own way through the years ahead. It is a safe haven for each of them to become their best self.

You are adding to your life not only the affection of each other, but also the companionship and blessing of a deep trust. You are agreeing to share strength, responsibilities, and love.

It takes more than love to make a relationship work. It takes trust to know in your hearts that you want only the best for each other. It takes dedication, to stay open to one another, to learn and grow, even when it is difficult to do so. And it takes faith, to go forward together into the mystery of what the future holds for you both.

One of the most powerful things you can do to keep your marriage vibrant and alive is to appreciate the big and the little things you do for each other every day.

Not to just think how much you appreciate the other, but to show it outwardly in what you say, and do. If you ever needed a challenge in your relationship, let it be a contest to see who can show their gratitude for the other the most.

Officiant to the couple: Challenge accepted?

Answer: Yes!

Officiant to the guests: Do you accept the challenge to be thankful for the people you love every day? If so, say, "We do!"

Answer: We do! We come now to the words [Couple's Names] want to hear the most today…the words that take them across the threshold from being engaged to being married.

Consent
Before you declare your vows to one another, do you confirm that it is indeed your freely given and gratefully offered intention to be married today? If so say, Yes.

Answer: Yes!

Vows and Ring Exchange

Officiant: Partner1, please repeat after me...

I, Partner1 take you, Partner2 to be my wife/husband. I appreciate and respect you for all you've done to fill my world with meaning. I promise to share my life openly with you, and build our dreams together. I will support you through times of trouble, and rejoice with you in times of happiness.

I promise to give thanks for you every day, to appreciate who you are and to tell you how much you mean to me. I make this commitment to you in love.

Ring is placed on Partner2's finger.
I give you this ring as a symbol of giving you my heart. Wear it with love and joy. As this ring has no end, my love is also forever.

Repeat for Partner 2.

Closing Blessing

May your life together be blessed with prosperity and good health. May you always share open and honest communication between each other. May you respect each other's individual talents and gifts and give full support to each other's professional and personal pursuits. May you cherish the home and family you will create together. May all the years to come be filled with moments to celebrate and renew your love. May your love be a life-long source of excitement, contentment, affection, respect, and devotion for one another.

[Couple's Names] thank you for your presence here today. They ask for your blessing, encouragement and lifelong support, for their marriage and life shared together.

Conclusion and Pronouncement

[Couple's Names] you have come here today of your own free will and in the presence of family and friends, have declared your appreciation, love and commitment to each other. You have given and received a ring as a symbol of your vows. By the power of your love and commitment to each other, and by the power vested in me, I now pronounce you married.

You may now share your first kiss as husband and wife.

Congratulations! Friends and family, I now present to you the newly married couple. Let's hear it for 'em!

A Bit of Dazzle

Because this ceremony is going to take place around a Thanksgiving meal, as a part of their vow exchange, the couple can offer each other a piece of bread, or piece of pie. A bit of humor can even be included by having them butter the bread for one another.

"I give you this piece of bread/pie as a token of my love and commitment."

They give each other a bite of bread, and then exchange their rings.

29 JUMPING THE BROOM

There's a great deal of history that informs the meaning of this ceremony. Jumping the Broom was the way unentitled slaves marked their marriage agreement. Slave owners could forbid marriage, exchanging rings, or holding a marriage ceremony, so the Broom ceremony used what was on hand and would be as inconspicuous as possible.

Today Jumping the Broom represents making a home together and leaving the past behind, sweeping out negativity, and starting a new life.

This ceremony can also be a great alternative to a traditional pronouncement. After the couple has Jumped the Broom, the officiant can introduce them as married.

Resources
See Link Directory

Script -- Traditional
Officiant: As [Couple's Names] jump, they physically and spiritually cross the threshold from being single and into two acting as one in marriage.

This ceremony marks the beginning of their making a home together. This event also symbolizes the sweeping away the old and welcoming the new.

By jumping the broom, the couple issues a call of support for the marriage from all of you here--their entire community of family and friends.

The leap they take together over the broom is also symbolic. By taking the leap, they make a gesture of dedication to working together through the tough times ahead, as well as the easy times.

They leave behind the past and jump into the future together, secure in their love.

[Couple's Names] will now begin their new life together with a clean sweep!

Everyone please count 1, 2, 3… jump together with me now, and shout with joy as they perform their first act of working together as husband and wife (or whatever their lifestyle preference is).

Group: 1, 2, 3, jump!

Optional: May I joyfully, with both feet on the ground, introduce to you for the first time as a married couple, [Couple's Names]!

A Bit of Dazzle

The following two versions of the ceremony were contributed by Officiant Patricia Burgess, Your Wedding, Your Way in Loganville, Georgia. Thank you, Patricia!

Jumping the Broom Including the Elders

While this version of Jumping the Broom includes the grandmothers, any elders the couple chooses can participate.

Officiant: We end this ceremony with the African American tradition of Jumping of the Broom. Slaves in this country were not permitted to marry, so they jumped a broom as a way of ceremonially uniting. Today it represents great joy and at the same time serves as a reminder of the past and the pain of slavery.

It is traditional that the elders of the family conduct the ritual. We therefore call up Partner1 and Partner2's grandmothers.

The broom is handed to the elder of one family, who makes sweeping gestures to eliminate any negative energies. That individual then hands the broom to the other elder representative, who places it on the ground in their path.

Officiant: As our bride and groom jump the broom, they physically and spiritually cross the threshold into their future. Today marks the beginning of formally making a home together. It symbolizes sweeping away the old and welcoming the new; sweeping away all negative energy, making way for all good things to come into their lives.

It is also a call of support for the marriage from the entire community of family and friends. The [Couple's Names] will now begin their new life together with a clean sweep!

Everyone count 1, 2, 3... Jump!
Together! 1, 2, 3... Jump!

Jumping the Broom to Sweep Out Prejudice and Negativity

Officiant: We end this ceremony with the African-American tradition of Jumping the Broom. As [Couple's Names] engage this ritual, they physically and spiritually cross the threshold into their marriage.

Traditionally, Jumping the Broom was also a means of sweeping away all negative energy, making way for all good things to come into their lives.

It is also a call of support for the marriage from the entire community of family and friends. In honoring the ritual, [Couple's Names] issue a hope and a prayer of sweeping away any hatred or prejudice between people of different colors, beliefs or traditions.

Partner2 and Partner1 will now begin their new life together with a clean sweep!

An attendant hands the broom to Partner2, who makes sweeping gestures to eliminate any negative energies. Partner2 then hands the broom to Partner1, who places it on the ground in their path.

Officiant: Everyone count 1, 2, 3... Jump! Together! 1, 2, 3... Jump!

More Bits of Dazzle

There are many different brooms that can be used, from a common broom to highly decorated brooms. Provide colorful ink pens and invite the guests to sign the handle as a memento for the couple.

Nehama Samson, Ketubah original art featured above on Etsy

This ceremony is a wonderful addition to a wedding because of the group nature it represents. Because of the wording between equals it's also a great addition to a modern ceremony. The way I have worded the following ceremony is my interpretation and is not the same as the way a rabbi would conduct the ceremony.

The Ketubah is considered an integral part of a traditional Jewish marriage ceremony. For non-Jews, they are also a work of art that conveys the meaningful sentiments in the text. Some of the examples on Etsy are gorgeous. The one featured here was hand made by Nehama Samson. She has many options of different styles, sizes and costs. I'm grateful for her generosity and talent.

Supplies
Easel or table for the Ketubah to be signed and or displayed
Ketubah's on Etsy. See Link Directory for Nehama Samson's storefront

Note: As in any ceremony that mentions children, always ask the couple if they want this section included.

The following is an example of the wording that's placed on a Ketubah plaque.

Officiant: A time honored tradition such as signing the Ketubah never loses its meaning when it comes from the heart. This plaque will forever bring back to [Couple's Names] the importance of this day and the love they committed to uphold, nurture and grow together. The following is an example of the wording that's placed on a Ketubah plaque. On the _____ day of the week, the _____ day of the month of _____, in the year 20____, which corresponds to the _____ day of the month in the _____ in the year 20____, (name of Partner1) daughter of (mother and father's name) and _____, (name of Partner2) son of (mother and father's name) entered into a mutual covenant, as equal partners before God and these witnesses and pledged to each other:

> "We will try always to be understanding and forgiving; sensitive to each other's needs and feelings.
> "We will be there for each other in times of need as in times of celebration.
> "We will share in each other's hopes and dreams and support each other to achievements great and small and through all of life's setbacks.

*"May the laughter of children grace the halls of our home.
"May we be poor in misfortune and rich in blessings.
"May the light of friendship guide our path together.
*"May we see our children's children.
"May the joy of living for one another bring smiles to our faces.
"May we know nothing but happiness from this day forward. "All of this we accept as valid and binding."

Signatures

Partner1 _____

Partner2 _____

Witness _____

Witness _____

Officiant _____

Officiant: "As we travel life's journey together, we will hold each other in respect, in admiration, and in love just as we will hold each other's hand."

A Bit of Dazzle

Because there's such a wide variety of Ketubahs available, a couple has many artistic and text options.

Does the couple have a graphically inventive friend? They can ask this person to design a Ketubah for their ceremony. The Ketubah is something that will be displayed on the wall. Because it's not a legal document it doesn't have a prescribed style or legend it has to conform to.

For example, the couple can draw a tree with roots going into the earth below. Guests can sign on the roots. In the example shown here, guests may sign in the leaves.

Another option is to show two favorite pets or animals that are surrounded by butterflies or stars. Each star or butterfly can be signed by a guest. If there are many guests, a few special people can be invited forward to sign and then they invite everyone to sign later and as the celebration unfolds.

Truly this is a tradition that makes room for a lot of imagination and creates quite a visual reminder of the love and support for the couple.

While signature lines are included in a traditional Ketubah, their witnesses and officiant, other guests can sign the Ketubah with a thumbprint or a little doodle that represents the person or family. They can sign their thumbprint or even make their names an artistic expression. Furnish a beautiful pen, or colored pens; something as artistic and special as the Ketubah being signed.

Love Locks photo courtesy of Ivan Kostyrya,
WoodbaobabUA, Kherson, Ukraine. Please support his Etsy site.

31 LOVE LOCKS

The Love Locks ceremony is a unique way of expressing the permanence of the couple's vows. For the couple who want a distinct way of honoring the commitment they are making, the key can be thrown away, showing there is no way to end their love because there's no way to unlock the Love Locks.

This special ceremony is a strong statement that the couple is making a lifelong, unbreakable commitment to each other forever. This ceremony can also include locks that the parents and other important people are asked to close/lock.

To see a ceremony in action: Simple Love Locks Ceremony

Supplies
The objects that the locks are locked on can also be beautiful art. Check out the many selections on Etsy. Or two locks can be locked to each other. The locks are the VIP of the ceremony. Locks can be engraved with the couple's names or a favorite word or short saying.

Love locks
Love lock tree, frame, or cords: On Etsy
Table for the frame or tree to sit on

Script

Optional: This first paragraph of the ceremony can include the parents. If there is a Love Lock Tree of Life the locks for parents typically are locked on the roots of the tree. If this part is included be sure the couple's tree frame has roots because all Love Lock trees do not have roots.

Officiant: Your parents have been the foundation that you've built your own life on, and so are the roots of the tree of your lives. Their love and joy have given you strength and support. They are represented by locks around these roots showing what a blessing they have been to your lives. You can close the lock now to show how your parents locked in such an important place in your lives.

Today you are joining your separate lives together. You are now holding a love lock which is a symbol of your commitment to one another. The message written on your love lock is the promise of love, acceptance, and unity.

The Love Lock Tree of Life represents all that you are and all that you'll ever be as an individual and a part of your union together. As you, [Couple's Names] lock your love lock to the Tree of Life, remember the reason you have come here today. Your love locks lock one time only. The absence of a key, (optional) symbolizes your commitment to each other for eternity. Your love is locked forever. As your life unfolds in its many directions, the branches will bear the celebrations of life to come because of the strength and durability of your commitment to one another.

Today you connect your two hearts together... your love will be forever.

Couple close the lock in the center of the Tree of Life or whatever their choice for the holder of the lock may be.

Officiant: [Couple's Names] the true key is in your hearts where the commitment you make to each other is built by respect, forgiveness, joy, and understanding. These are the Keys to Love:

Reading: Keys to Love

The key to love is understanding...the ability to comprehend not only the spoken word, but those unspoken gestures, the little things that say so much by themselves.

The key to love is forgiveness...to accept each other's faults and pardon mistakes, without forgetting, but with remembering what you learn from them.

The key to love is sharing...facing your good fortunes as well as the bad, together; conquering problems, forever searching for ways to intensify your happiness.

The key to love is giving...without thought of return, but with the hope of just a simple smile, and by giving in but never giving up.

The key to love is respect...realizing that you are two separate people, with different ideas; that you don't belong to each other, that you belong with each other, and share a mutual bond.

The key to love is inside us all...It takes time and patience to unlock all the ingredients that will take you to its threshold; it is the continual learning process that demands a lot of work...but the rewards are more than worth the effort...and those are the keys to love.

Blessing
May these keys to love always be in your heart and mind and the commitment you make to each other today give your heart the freedom to love each other foolishly, compassionately, and well.

Bits of Dazzle
The key to the love locks can be attached to two bio-degradable, helium-filled balloons and released as a final part of this ceremony.

The keys can be buried, or locked within the locks themselves so it can be seen but never used.

32 LOVING CUP AND MEAD

The first time I did this ceremony the groom and his groomsmen were dressed in kilts and talkin' in brogue. The bride walked in with bagpipes playing and when they recessed as husband and wife, the bagpipes came back to life. The entire experience was quite majestic and seeing those men standing at the altar decked out in Scottish finery created the feeling we were all in Scotland. Another nice touch was the groom had brewed the mead which, when he let me sample it after the ceremony, had a surprisingly sweet taste. Mead is made with honey so a sweet flavor makes sense.

Depending on the current state of health guidelines, some couples like to pass the mead to their attendants and/or family members.

In the Script when the Loving Cup is referred to, this includes either the Loving or Marriage Cup.

Supplies
Mead

If including other participants, have at least a gallon of mead. Otherwise, a pint or quart should do.

A simple mead recipe comes from **Grow, Forage, Cook, Ferment**. See Link Directory

Loving Cup* or Marriage Cup**

Table on which to place the Loving Cup and Mead

Background
* If using a Loving Cup: Here's a theory as to why it's called a Loving Cup. John Wesley, (1703-1781), founder of the Methodist church, hosted 'loving feasts', where a cup of water was shared with everyone present. The cup he passed had two handles making it easier to pass from person to person, hence the name "loving cup". Pictured Loving Cup made by

** If using a Marriage Cup: A Marriage Cup reminds me of the Native American Wedding Vase. It's a double drinking vessel with a skirt-shaped large cup which is for the groom and a small swivel cup is for the bride. The idea is to drink the contents at the same time, making sure not to spill even a drop.

Script

Officiant: The purpose of the Celtic Loving Cup and Mead Ceremony is for [Couple's Names] to share their first drink together as a married couple and to show the coming together of two families.

The cup is then passed down from generation to generation, ensuring happiness and good fortune to all who drink from it. This is a special moment for [Couple's Names] to toast their love, devotion, and friendship.

Their years of life together are as a cup of mead poured out for you to drink. This Loving Cup contains within it mead with certain properties that are sweet and symbolic of happiness, joy, hope, peace, love, and delight.

This same mead also holds some bitter properties that are symbolic of disappointment, sorrow, grief, despair, and life's trials and tribulations. Together the sweet and the bitter represent love's journey and all of the experiences that are a natural part of it.

Optional: For all who share the mead from this Loving Cup, so may you share all things from this day on with love and understanding. Those who drink deeply from the Loving Cup with an open heart and willing spirit, invite the full range of challenges and experiences into their being for themselves and the [Couples Names].

If using the Marriage Cup, individual cups will have to be used by those also drinking the mead. It's highly suggested that even if it's a Loving Cup that's used, individual cups are used. The best man, maid of honor, or the officiant can pour the mead into individual cups and then hand them out to participants.

Officiant pours mead into the Loving Cup and holds it up.

This cup of mead is symbolic of the cup of life. As you all share the mead from the Loving Cup, you undertake to share all that the future may bring. It represents a blessing of love and peace for each person participating in this ceremony. All the sweetness life's cup may hold for each of you will be the sweeter because you drink it together. Whatever drops of bitterness it may contain will be less bitter because you share them. Drink now, and may the cup of your lives be sweet and full to running over.

Officiant *holds up the Loving Cup and says:* This Loving Cup is symbolic of the pledges you have made to one another to share together the fullness of life. As you drink from this cup, you acknowledge to one another that your lives, separate until this moment, have now become one.

Officiant *hands the Loving Cup to Partner1 and Partner2 and says:* Now drink to the love you've shared in the past. *Couple sips from the Loving Cup.*

Officiant: Drink to your love in the present, on your wedding day. *Couple sips from the Loving Cup.*

Officiant: And drink to your love in the future and forevermore! *Couple sips from the Loving Cup and hand it back to the Officiant.*

Officiant: As you have shared the mead from this Loving Cup, may you generously share your lives. May you explore the mysteries of the Loving Cup and share in the reflection of love in one another's soul. All life flows from love and back to love it must return. May you find life's joys heightened, its bitterness sweetened, and all of life enriched by the love of family and friends.

Couple return to their place before the officiant.

A Bit of Dazzle
Have the recipe for the mead printed out to give to guests or include it as part of the wedding ceremony program.

33 MARRIAGE BETWEEN EQUALS

This is a short ceremony that recognizes the equality of both partners, setting the intention that one partner isn't more powerful or important than the other, nor is one partner relegated to a role without full consent. This ritual acknowledges each partner's individuality. These are two people giving 100% to keep their relationship interesting, alive, and growing. This is not a ceremony for the couple who wants to commit 50%/50% because it implies either one of the partners can back off rather than two individuals walking equally side by side.

I remember the first couple who asked me to make a point of calling out their commitment to be equal partners. They didn't want to leave any doubt that theirs was not going to be a marriage where one was the head of the household and the other would be subservient to the other. They also made the point to family and friends that they believed marriage equality should extend to same sex marriages as well.

This ceremony is the result of their request.

Historical perspective

Most biblical scholars would agree that the idea the man is more consequential than woman comes from Eve being created from Adam's rib. In other words, since she didn't come from the same raw material as Adam, she must be less important. However, rib means "living" in Hebrew, from a root that can also mean "snake". A long-standing exegetical tradition holds that the use of a rib from man's side emphasizes that both man and woman have equal dignity, for woman was created from the same material as man, shaped and given life by the same processes. In fact, since Eve was created from the best form God had, Eve was a new and improved model. Think on that for a minute!

Set up

There needs to be enough room for the couple to take a few steps side to side. This ceremony may fit in well at the beginning of the larger ceremony or after they exchange their vows. If either one of the partners wears a dress with a long train, the steps taken in the ceremony may not be necessary. They can simply turn one way or the other.

Script

Officiant: There may be those of us here who were raised to honor the male above the female. Controlling others was more important than being in control of oneself.

[Couple's Names] live by the truth that [Partner1] is not less nor more important than [Partner2]. That their desires are equally essential and their priorities are equally important. They honor each other as both a follower and leader, a giver and a receiver. They seek to talk with each other and not at one another and to build their friendship so it is a source of strength, comfort and wisdom.

To live as equals can change our world a better place one expression of respect at a time. Not only does the love that [Couple's Names] have found improve our world because of their commitment to love, but they know they can show the world that so much joy comes from living as equals rather than one being regarded as better that the other.

Reading

> Don't walk in front of me... I may not follow
> Don't walk behind me... I may not lead
> Walk beside me... just be my friend
>
> Albert Camus*

Officiant: This is the walk that two equal partners in marriage may do. *Ask the couple to face each other.*

Officiant: This is how equals face each other. *Direct Partner1 to turn away from Partner2.*

Officiant: Don't walk in front of me, I may not follow. But I can choose to follow. Will you respect one another and follow when following is called for?

Couple answers: Yes.

Direct the couple to take two steps forward, then 2 steps back and face each other again. Pause. Direct Partner2 to turn away from Partner1.

Officiant: Don't walk behind me, I may not lead. But I may choose to lead. Will you respect one another and lead one another?

Couple answers: Yes.

Invite them to take two steps forward, then 2 steps back. Direct the couple to face the officiant.

Officiant: Walk beside me ... just be my friend. Do you promise to nurture each other so this is a marriage between equals?

Couple answers: Yes.

Officiant: Then it is so. *Couple can kiss each other's hands.*

Ceremony proceeds.

A Bit of Dazzle

Washing each other's feet may be a bit too Christian for some couples and is also cumbersome though symbolic and quite touching. Washing each other's hands rather than kissing each other's hands at the end can emphasize the element of serving each other.

If this dazzle is used, the couple will need to have a shallow bowl of warm water, a wash cloth and hand towel. One of the attendants can place the bowl on a table set up for this option. Note that having just a small amount of water will help to minimize splashing any water on a beautiful wedding gown.

Script

Officiant: [Couple's Names] seek to further confirm their desire to live as equals by washing each other's hands. Our hands are symbolic of service and dedication. Washing is the symbol of cleansing, of being clear on their commitment to make this a marriage between equals.

Do you seek to serve one another?

Are you ready to let go of the old ideas of one being better than the other, of compromising your values in order to accommodate the other, only to build resentment?

Couple answers: Yes.

Direct the couple to stand at the table with the bowl of water, washcloth and towel. Instruct Partner1 to take the washcloth, dip it in the bowl and gently wash Partner2's hands. Then gently dry the hands.

Repeat for Partner2 washing Partner1's hands.

Couple steps back to the officiant and the ceremony proceeds.

* Albert Camus was a French philosopher, author, and journalist He had a great sense of style, and was even asked to pose for Vogue. He was quite down to earth and fun. In 1957, he was awarded the Nobel Prize in Literature at the age of 44, the second-youngest recipient in history.)

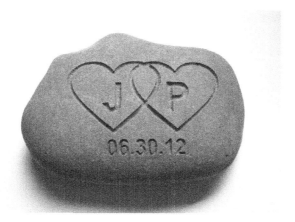

Photo, Monkeys Jewels, Etsy.com

34 OATHING STONE

This is one of those ceremonies I've never actually done. I love the idea of it and have pieced this ceremony together based on research with Officiant Google and a bit of intuition. This ceremony is fairly simple and the setup is what takes the most effort.

I'd love to receive any stories and experiences from you if you've lead this ceremony.

Supplies

A stone suitable for use as an Oathing stone.

> The stone can be the size of a brick or as large as a stepping stone.
> The stone can be collected by the couple at a favorite place where they often hike, have visited, from a beach, etc.

Small stones if guests are going to participate. See *A Bit of Dazzle*.

> Option: The Oathing stone can have their wedding date chiseled in it, their initials, a favorite saying, or a symbol they connect with.

Table to hold the Oathing Stone

Resources

Etsy has many storefronts for Oathing stones. The stones pictured here are from Dean McKinnon of Monkey's Jewels. See Link Directory.

Special consideration

The Oathing Stone can set up on a table before the ceremony OR it can be brought forward by a Person of Importance. But the Stone will need to be brought forward and placed in front of the officiant and the couple step to opposite sides of the Stone so their backs aren't to their guests. The table can be moved by one of the attendants or the Person of Importance can hold the stone while they share their vows.

Script

Officiant: As [Couple's Names] prepare to share their vows, they're using the Scottish tradition of the Oathing stone.

Would [Person of Importance] come forward with the Stone please?

Stone is held by the Person of Importance or they bring the table to the couple.

For those of you not familiar with this old Scottish tradition, [Couple's Names] will place (or hold) their hands together on the Oathing Stone as they repeat their wedding vows. Some believe that this ceremony is where the phrase "set in stone" comes from.

[Couple's Names] will now say their wedding vows to each other. Couple shares their own written vows or may repeat after the officiant.

A Bit of Dazzle

It's not uncommon for the guests to receive a small stone when they arrive which as you'll see, adds to the group dynamic of this ceremony.

Dazzle Script

Officiant: When you arrived, you were given a stone to hold in your hand during the wedding ceremony. [Couple's Names] chose these stones as symbols of your special relationship, love, good wishes and heartfelt blessings to them. The stones will serve as a lasting reminder of your presence at their wedding and of the special love that they shared on this their special day. t chapter two text here.

As you hold the stone tightly in your hand, please reflect for a moment your wishes for this couple for love, happiness, prosperity, and unity as they exchange their wedding vows.   Following the ceremony, [Couple's Names] invite you to throw the stones with your personal blessing for them as a newly married couple into the water to wish them all the best in their married life together.

Double Dazzle

The couple can make their own Oathing stone from concrete and decorate it with meaningful objects such as charms, special stones, semi-precious jewels,   etc.

Photo, Vanya Kostyria, Etsy.com

35 PUZZLE

I love doing this ceremony because it's so unique and can be quite "artsy.". The idea of missing pieces in our couple's experience coming together to form a whole picture in such a visual way can be very meaningful.

Getting this ceremony together takes a bit of extra effort if the couple wants a puzzle that's made especially for them. The puzzle can be easily made by a woodworker in the family, and people can even take a photo of the two of them, fix it to a piece of thin plywood and have the puzzle cut out for them.

Supplies
Personalized Puzzle. The heart puzzle pictured is available on Etsy from our Ukrainian craftsman. See Link Directory.

Script
Officiant: In life we can look around feeling like things don't quite fit together. We search for the missing pieces. And then one day, two people meet and they seem to fit together. What they bring to the relationship fills out the picture, completes the circle, pulls the past and present together in a way that begins to reveal the larger picture. The future is symbolized by the picture becoming whole.

Option

Officiant: The puzzle [Couple's Names] have chosen to put together today represents their coming together to fill out the bigger-picture. The puzzle contains many different sizes and shapes which also symbolizes the unique experience of different times of their life, and of their families and friends. When the individual pieces are brought together by trial and error and finally recognizing where each piece belongs, the result is a complete circle.

While today celebrates your union as a married couple, your assembling this puzzle doubles as a dedication to the bond and love of this family as a whole.

As each of you place your puzzle piece, you display your dedication to the family and your commitment to always keep the different and unique parts of your family together. To keep the whole as one. From this day onward, may you enjoy the pieces of the puzzle and embrace the love and completeness of your life together as a family.

Couple puts pieces together and / or Officiant invites others to come join them in putting the puzzle together.

Couple return to their place with the officiant.

Photos courtesy of Ivan Kostyrya, Owner of WoodbaobabUA on Etsy. Ivan is from Ukraine and sells personalized gifts that reflect Family values, Personalized Gifts, Wedding Gifts, Couples Gifts, Anniversary Gifts, Wedding Puzzles.

A Bit of Dazzle plus

If someone in the family is a woodworker this adds extra meaning to the puzzle and a story can be told about how this person has inspired the couple because of the creative work of his or her hands.

A non-wedding dazzle – if you're with a group of people and you've finished a big project together, this ceremony can be a way to show how everyone contributed to the project.

36 RECOMMITMENT OR VOW RENEWAL

I love recommitment ceremonies. It's so encouraging to know people love each other more than ever after a long period of time. Sometimes a married couple wants a vow renewal ceremony after the children are grown and as adults, the parents want them included in the ceremony. Sometimes children are younger, or graduating from high school. Whatever their choices are, their love and respect for each other is an honor to be around.

The following is a long ceremony and as a rule, I only use parts of it. I think one of the things we learn as we become more experienced at officiating is that we pick up on the cues that what we're saying isn't making an impression. It's interesting to note that in 2021 the average human attention span has fallen from 12 seconds in 2000 to eight seconds today.

Supplies
Rings whether current or new wedding rings
Flower if Flower Exchange option is chosen

Script
Officiant: We are here today to celebrate your marriage and to be present for the recommitment of your love for one another.

Even though this is a private ceremony, those who adore you are happy that you continue to love each other in such a powerful and tender way and there's no hiding your love for each other from your family. Your love binds you all together, giving dignity, meaning, worth, and appreciation for the big and little things of life that brighten your days.

You are about to declare your very special love and reaffirm your lasting commitment as partners in love for life. The promises you're about to make, affirm your continuing love to be a special commitment which will continue to strengthen your lives and prepare you for whatever situations you may face with the strength and courage of two.

Again, you're committing to the love you know for each other in an unselfish giving to one another; not in the attitude of duty or sacrifice, but in the spirit of joy. You accept each other totally, creating a safe and loving space for each other to grow as individuals and partners and to mature in the faith and unshakable trust you have for each other.

Reflections

[Couple's Name] when you first joined hands and hearts in (year they were married), you didn't know where love would lead you. You promised to love, honor and cherish one another through all things. Life has brought you both wonderful blessings as well as the challenges that come with two people joining in their commitment not to just care for and serve one another but to make a commitment to know what love is. You have fulfilled your promises. And today you set out upon the journey to fulfill your promise in new ways!

Would you agree that love is more than verses on Valentine's cards and romance in movies?

Love is here and now, real and true, the most important thing in your lives. For love is the creator of your favorite memories and the foundation of your fondest dreams.

Without love, you merely exist. With love, you truly begin to live!

For love is a promise that is always kept, a fortune that can never be spent, a seed that can flourish in even the most unlikely place. And this radiance that never fades; this mysterious and magical joy is the greatest treasure of all - one known only by those who truly love.

Someone once said: "The most wonderful of all things in life is the discovery of another human being with whom one's relationship has a growing depth, beauty and joy as the years increase."

This inner progressiveness of love between two human beings is a most marvelous thing; it cannot be found by looking for it or by passionately wishing for it. It's a Divine destiny.

Charge to the Couple

Happiness in marriage is not something that just happens. A good marriage must be created. In the art of marriage, the little things are the big things.

It is never being too old to hold hands.
It is remembering to say, "I love you" out loud, at least once a day.
It is never going to sleep angry.
It is forming a circle of love that gathers in the whole family.
It is at no time taking the other for granted. . . for what you take for granted, disappears.
It is speaking words of appreciation and demonstrating gratitude in thoughtful ways.
It is having the capacity to forgive and not bring it up later.
It is giving each other an atmosphere in which each can grow.
It is not expecting Partner2 to wear a halo or Partner1 to have the wings of an angel.
It is not looking for perfection in each other.
It's cultivating flexibility, patience, understanding and a sense of humor.
It is a common search for the good and the beautiful in each other.
It is not only marrying the right partner, it's BEING the right partner.

Marriage can be a great adventure when it's the outward expression of a great love; such a love is characterized by compassion, passion and courage.

Your love requires that you be totally honest with yourself and your mate, that you ask for what you want, take action even though you are afraid, share your feelings and listen but leave your partner free to be who he/she really is. In other words, always love your partner for who they are, not for who you think they should be.

Officiant: Please face each other. Remembering your wedding vows made [number of years] ago on [date and year of wedding day] is it your intention that you now affirm new vows?

Both: Yes, it is.

Partner1, I love you differently than the love I had for you on our wedding day. I want you to know that my love and commitment to you is even stronger than it was because of what we've shared together. I love you more with each passing day.

Partner2, I love you differently than the love I had for you on our wedding day. I want you to know that my love and commitment to you is even stronger than it was because of what we've shared together. I love you more with each passing day.

Partner2, please repeat after me:
I, Partner2, promise to continue to love, cherish and protect you Partner1 whose hand I now hold, and provide for in health and sickness, and to be true and faithful to you. I say these words because I love you, and choose to continue to live the rest of my life with you. I renew my vow to honor and respect you as my wife/husband.

Partner1, please repeat after me:
I, Partner1, promise to continue to love, cherish and protect you Partner2 whose hand I now hold, and provide for in health and sickness, and to be true and faithful to you. I say these words because I love you, and choose to continue to live the rest of my life with you. I renew my vow to honor and respect you as my wife/husband.

Optional – Flower exchange
Officiant: Your gift to each other on your wedding day was your wedding rings - which will always be an outward demonstration of your vows of love and respect; and a public showing of your commitment to each other.

Today, your promise of renewal comes in the form of a single red rose bud. The rose is considered a symbol of love and a single rose always means only one thing - it says the words "I love you."

Within these roses, if given proper loving care, is the potential for an even more beautiful expression of Life and Love in the form of the mature flower just like your marriage.

May that special love you now share continue to grow and blossom in the years to come and be sustained by the Divine, by family and friends and by the commitment you make again this day. May you find in each other companionship as well as love, understanding as well as compassion, challenge as well as agreement.

Optional-- New Anniversary Ring Exchange
Officiant: What symbols do you give to reaffirm this marriage?

Couple: These rings.
Officiant: Your rings are circles and a circle is the symbol of the sun, the earth, the universe, of wholeness, perfection, peace and unity. Like circles, your rings have no beginning and no ending.

Let each of us in our own way, may it be a prayer, a thought, or whatever you and I would wish for this couple, let's pray or have our own thoughts as a blessing on these rings. Let's pause at this time for these silent blessings. (pause) These rings, now blessed are a symbol of love and faithfulness.

Officiant to Partner2: Please repeat after me.
I give you this ring as a symbol of my continuing love and devotion, and with all that I am, and all that I have today, tomorrow, and forever.

You may place the ring on Partner1's finger.

Officiant to Partner1: Please repeat after me.
I give you this ring as a symbol of my continuing love and devotion, and with all that I am, and all that I have today, tomorrow, and forever.

You can place the ring on Partner2's finger.

Alternative Ring Blessing Ceremony

Your rings, though unique, are similar to the unknown numbers of all those who have come before you in marriage. Most certainly the shared and universal desire to love and be loved without conditions is represented first and foremost by these rings.

Your rings are circles. A circle is the symbol of the sun and of the earth, and of the universe. The rings you give and receive this day are a symbol of the circle of shared love, without beginning and without end.

They are made of precious metals, which are symbolic of the strength and durability of your relationship. The jewels represent the joy and the beauty of your love.

Blessing

May the home in which you live continue be an island where the pressures of the world can be sorted out and brought into focus; where tensions can be released and understood; where personal needs do not tower over concern for others and where the warmth of humor and love puts crisis into perspective. And above all, may you find an even richer joy in living, learning and loving together.

Pronouncement of Marriage

Now that you have reaffirmed your love and commitment to each other by your new vows, with the joining of hands and the giving and receiving of a red rose bud, I affirm that you are wonderfully married, in the name of all that is good, pure and true

Optional Introduction of Couple

Congratulations [Couple's Name]. May the next [number of years] years be more wonderful than your first [years married]. No matter what surprises there may be, love is why you are together.

Go in peace. Continue to enjoy the wonder and power of your Love!

Jim and Catherine, 40-year anniversary recommitment

A Bit of Dazzle

Recommitment ceremonies are often very private, with few guests, or a wedding photographer. Take a few photos of the location, any interesting markers or signs that mark the location, and photos of the couple and any guests. Prepare a collage of the pictures you took of the event, have it framed, and present the collection to your couple.

37 RING WARMING

Background

This tradition originated in Ireland, but ring warmings are practiced in contemporary and traditional weddings all over the world. Either the officiant or designated leader passes the rings among the guests. However, someone in the wedding party must be responsible for keeping track of where the rings are so when the times comes for the couple to exchange their rings the are readily retrievable! Check out A Bit of Dazzle for a few suggestions for passing the rings among guests.

One of the nice things about the Ring Warming Ceremony is it gives friends and family a chance to be involved. More and more, interactive moments in a ceremony are being incorporated, and this is one of those opportunities.

Considerations

Explain the process for this ceremony before the couple share their vows so there's plenty of time for the ring to be passed around and ready for their exchange of rings.

If there are more than twenty guests it may be more of a challenge to retrieve the rings in a timely fashion before the officiant begins this ceremony. Instead, consider making the attendants the only ones who participate in the ring warming. DO give a larger group of guests the opportunity to silently warm it up "with a prayer, wish or good thoughts."

Last but not least, decide who the officiant will receive the warmed rings from such as the Best Man. He is in charge of knowing where the rings are among the guests.

Photo of rings by Sandy Millar on Unsplash
#thetinycelebrant

Script

Officiant: [Couple's Name] are about to exchange their vows and rings.

(Directed to the guests) You are here today because you mean so much to these two, and truth be told, you have had quite a bit to do with them becoming who they needed to be in order to find each other.

[Couple's Name] would love for you to take the rings they are about to exchange and hold them in your hand when they're passed to you.

As you offer a silent blessing, wish, a prayer, or good thoughts as you hold the rings in your hand, you'll be "warming" the rings with your good energy. You don't have to hold the rings for a long time for your prayers and wishes to warm these rings. What's most important is when [Couple's Name] wear their rings, your best wishes will carry an energy that blesses their relationship forever.

To the group: When you've finished, please carefully pass the rings to the next person.

When everyone has had a chance to bless the rings, if the last person to have the rings will raise his or her hand, and [Designated Person's Name] will come fetch them and bring them forward for the ring exchange.

Officiant places the rings in the preferred container and hands the container to the attendants who then pass the ring into the congregation for the guests to "warm" it up. Ring is passed around, and returned to the officiant.

Officiant to the couple: Now that these rings have been blessed and filled by the love of your family and friends, your rings are ready to exchange. Remember how these loving people here only want the best for you today, and for your entire lives together.

Vow and Ring exchange proceeds.

A Bit of Dazzle

Pass the rings around in a special bowl or box and add the facts to the directions the officiant gives guests before the rings are passed around.

Instead of passing the rings around, hang the rings on ribbons which hand from a small potted tree, a wreath, heart, or symbol the couple relates to. Appoint someone to direct folks what to do when they enter, which is bless the rings on the tree or wreath, heart, or symbol.

When the officiant receives the rings back from the person retrieving them, lead the guests in the affirmation, "The Love within us has blessed your rings and will keep you warm in Divine Love forever."

38 SAGE SMUDGING

Background

The ritual of sage burning has its roots in Native American tradition. Many people use this tradition and burn sage and other herbs to cleanse a space or environment of negative energy, to generate wisdom and clarity, and to promote healing. When we smudge in a wedding ceremony, the officiant should smudge her/himself as part of the opening of the ceremony, or smudge themselves before the ceremony begins.

Understanding the history of a ceremony we undertake can pave the way for kind of collective letting go. Our willingness and sincerity in leading this ceremony whether we're indigenous American or not, engages the power of the ceremony. If this process seems silly or has no meaning for the officiant then I don't recommend it. "Your faith has made you whole" can be applied to "Your belief in this activity makes it effective." In other words, what we have faith in is imbued with energy and this is why sage smudging can be cleansing for the participants as they let go of their old life and enter a new one together.

Supplies

Abalone shell or fireproof pottery bowl to hold the smoking materials, if using loose leaves
White, or blue sage*, cedar, sweet grass or herbs such as lavender or mugwort
Feather or plume for wafting
Matches

*White sage is a fairly common variety of sage that's used for space clearing. But the officiant can also use bundles of cedar or herbs like mugwort. Whatever material you choose, the ceremony is based most on the couple's intention for clearing out the old and making way for the new. Ideally, look for a source that harvests its herbs ethically and responsibly.

Process

Smudging is done with a bundle of sage wrapped with twine. Small bundles can be lit on the end, and used to smudge. A larger bundle can be split up into loose leaf and used. In this case, place a handful of sage in a shell or bowl, light the material, and carefully allow the flame to go out so that the tips of the dried leaves are smoldering slowly. Let the smoke rise and wave the feather or plume to spread the smoke into the area for cleansing. If necessary, blow on the smoldering end to release more smoke and fan the smolder, but keep your face far away (at least two feet), because sometimes little sparks of ash break off, and you don't want them flying in your face.

You can get expressive with your fanning, but always remain conscious of the fact that you're holding a burning object. If you see fallen ashes, put them out immediately.

Usually the smudging is done at the very start of the ceremony or just before the couple shares their vows. This ceremony is written for the beginning of the exchange of vows.

Smudging the officiant (optional)

1. Light the material until there is a small waft of smoke coming from the bowl or bundle.
2. If you have glasses, smudge glasses and take them off so that nothing can get in the way of the energy meant for your eyes.
3. Run your hands through the smoke and rub your hands in the smoke as if you were cleansing them with soap.
4. Pull the smoke towards you to smudge your breath and place you hand briefly on your mouth.
5. Smudge your eyes and ears, and then place your hands over your hands briefly on your eyes and then your ears.
6. Run your hands through the smoke again and then over your hair, your ears, heart, and your feet, making sure you have your hands in the smoke frequently. When you have smudged your whole body, say a little prayer to be of service to your couple and to their family and friends.

Smudging the Couple

If needed, place more material in the bowl, or blow on the stick to keep the smudge going.

Officiant: Sage smudging is done in order to cleanse the environment of any negative energy, fear, or doubt, and to generate in its place wisdom, clarity, and promote healing. Smoke symbolizes the rising of our awareness heavenward, to a higher consciousness.

Officiant faces the couple and uses her/his hand, feather or plume to push the smoke in a circle above, below and encircling the couple.

Officiant: We cleanse the energy around you so that you are surrounded only by the love.

Officiant smudges towards the couple's face. Continue to wave the smoke towards the couple as long as you are in the area being mentioned in your words.

Note: The couple can cup their hands and pull the smoke toward themselves.

Officiant: We smudge your breath so that in your marriage, you may hear the sacred words and expressions of love you say about and to one another. We smudge your eyes so you can see all the good things you share in your life together. We smudge your hair because it contains the DNA of your individual histories and you may share this DNA with your offspring.

Officiant moves the bowl or bundle lower on the couple's bodies and wafts the smudge on them.

Officiant: We smudge the heart to cleanse it of past hurts and open your creative center to the wonder and power of the love you share.

Couple pulls smoke towards their heart and then places their hands over their hearts.

Officiant walks around the couple: We offer the sacred smoke to you to cleanse your body so it is strong and healthy and you live many, many happy years together.

Officiant waves the smoke towards their feet.

We smudge your feet so you may walk on the earth with great respect.

(Optional) Closing Prayer

May you feel the presence of our Great Creator who is with [Couple's Names] always. Today is a beautiful day and any negativity and doubt has been cleansed. We are grateful. And so it is.

Officiant: Are you ready to make your vows? Answer: Yes!

Proceed with the vows and ring exchange.

A Bit of Dazzle

Once the sage is lit, the couple can smudge each other while the officiant narrates what's going on. This is a great option as there's a lot of script to memorize.

As the couple moves from one area to the next or if they choose to only do one sweeping circle of smudging, the officiant can lead the guests in affirming "Yes" or "A Ho" (Yes in Cherokee).

Begin the ceremony with sage smudging and end with the Arches Ceremony.

39 SAKE SHARING

Background

San-san-kudo is a Japanese Sake (rice wine) sharing ceremony and is common in Japanese weddings. San-san-kudo—*san* means "three," *ku* means "nine," and *do* means "to deliver." The current Shinto (and Buddhist) wedding style started around 120 years ago and began with the Japanese Emperor's wedding. Not only are wedding vows and rings exchanged, but also cups of sacred Sake are exchanged between the couple and their families.

Sake is a brewed beverage (as opposed to distilled) which is made from rice. The process used to make Sake is called "multiple parallel fermentation". This means the conversion of starch to sugar happens at the same time as sugar to alcohol, which does not happen in any other alcoholic beverage. Creating the beverage from the rice takes about three weeks, and the fermentation process can last up to four months.

Sometimes a couple who incorporate Buddhist teachings into their lifestyle may appreciate this ceremony. A couple doesn't have to be Asian to use the Sake Sharing ceremony. The theme of this ritual is affirming the unity of the couple and their parents.

Process

The couple takes three sips of Sake from three stacked cups. After your twosome sip their Sake, both sets of parents also sip the Sake. The ritual is complete after a total of nine sips. Nine (ku) is a lucky number in Japanese; the phrase *san-san-kudo* translates literally to "three, three, nine times." *Sharing Sake created a formal bond as strongly as a handshake did in Victorian times.*

To begin, the officiant pours Sake in each of the three bowls. Be sure to pour an amount that isn't easily spilled.

Script

Officiant: [Couple's Names] and their parents are going to take part in the San-san-kudo ceremony. By drinking Sake from the same cup, the couple is firmly united as husband and wife and with their families. There are three types of Sake cups: the small cup represents their past. In the middle is the medium cup which signifies their present. Their future is symbolized by the large cup.

Officiant to [Couple's Names]: This small cup represents the three couples: [Couple's Names], Partner1's parents, and Partner2's parents.

Sip from the small cup and repeat after me "I'm grateful for my ancestors who raised me and for the past that I have met."

Partner1 and Partner2 repeat and take a sip from the small cup. They pass the cup to Partner1's parents who take a sip, then pass to Partner2's parents who take a sip from the small cup. The cup is passed back to the officiant who sets it on the table.

Pause.

Officiant: Sip from the medium cup which represents human love, wisdom, and happiness which you enjoy today, and repeat after me, "My aspiration is to marry and work together with my mate/life partner."

Partner1 and Partner2 take a sip from the medium cup and passes it to Partner1's parents who take a sip, then passes it to Partner2's parents who take a sip from the medium cup. The cup is passed back to the officiant who sets it on the table.

Pause.

Officiant: Sip now from the large cup which represents family and the unknown future, and repeat after me: "We wish to build a happy family and pledge eternal love."

Partner1 and Partner2 take a sip from the large cup and they pass it to Partner1's parents who take a sip, then pass it to Partner2's parents who take a sip from the large cup. The cup is passed back to the officiant who sets it on the table.

Officiant: It is our greatest hope that your past, present and future are filled with love, respect and devotion to each other and to family.

Everyone bows to the other. Parents are seated and couple returns to the altar.

A Bit of Dazzle

If there is any family history behind the cups or the kind of Sake that is chosen, let this be part of the introduction to the ceremony.

Suggest the couple make Sake available if there is a bar at the reception.

Jim and Mandi Peterson

40 CLASSIC SAND

The Sand Ceremony is one of the most popular ceremonies and for good reason – strong visual symbolism that adds meaning and personality to the ceremony. It's wonderful when the officiant can include a story about where the sand came from and why that's important to the couple. The story can be a funny anecdote, super serious, or both.

Etsy.com and brick and mortar stores like Michaels and Joann's usually carry Sand Ceremony kits. Sand vessels may be picture frames, hourglasses, Ball jars, salad dressing cruets, or containers specifically designed for the Sand Ceremony. I always encourage my couples to choose a central vase that has a wide enough neck so it's not difficult for the couple and/or family members to pour the sand into it. One of my favorite kits was a central vase that could be turned into an oil burning lamp.

If the couple collects sand from a favorite beach for the ceremony, encourage them to dry the sand before using it so the sand doesn't clump. Instead of pouring smoothly, wet sand spits and plops.

Most importantly, make the point that the end product is totally unique. Just like they are.

Couple's Sand Ceremony

Officiant: [Couple's Names], your marriage not only joins you together as a couple, it joins your two families together in very unique and special relationships. In this bond, each of you may share many experiences as if you are one person. You'll share celebrations, and times of loss and grief. But while you will share life's unfoldment together, you never lose your own identity. The miracle of love is that it allows us to overcome any sense of isolation, yet continues to affirm our individuality.

These two colors of sand symbolize [Couple's Names] separate lives, and (looking at your couple) the separate families that you bring here today. The merging of your two sands into one indicates your desire that your lives, and the lives of your families and friends, be joined as one.

Optional: Ask the gathered group: Is it your wish to come together as one with [Couple's Names]? If so, say together, "Yes", "Woo hoo!" or "You betcha!"

Officiant to the couple: Take your individual vials of sand and pour them into the large single container.

Sand is poured. NOTE: couples don't always know whether they should pour their sand separately or together. Personally, I like it poured together.)

There is no other pattern or shape, form, or color like what you've just created. It's true of your relationship as well. Your marriage is unique. We hope that what you've created here reminds you that you do not have to follow in anyone else's footsteps, but must make your own choices, your own mistakes, and take your own journey into happiness and peace.

All of us here, have a wish for you--that you will continuously blend your families with love, sharing, and happiness, so that there is always new light and joy, peace and harmony in your hearts and all of your homes.

A Bit of Dazzle
See the 10 Ways to Add Dazzle to the Sand Ceremony.

41 FAMILY SAND

Set up

Children should choose a color of sand in their favorite color.

To help a younger child remember which vial is theirs, put a little sticker with their name on the back of the vessel they're going to use.

Couple approaches the altar table and stand behind it so their guests can see them.

Script

Officiant: As you look at these containers of sand, know each one represents the essence of all that you are and all that you bring to your marriage. Bring to mind the strength of your vows, the honesty and integrity with which you made them, and all the particles of personality that make you unique and wonderful in each other's eyes.

Couple stand behind the altar so guests can see their faces. Each takes their container of sand in hand.

Within a marriage, each person is both their own and each other's. They are wo individuals choosing to create a new life with endless possibilities and new dreams that are theirs together. Now it's time to pour the sand into the vessel that represents the foundation of your love, supports, and nurtures your marriage and your family.

Couple intermingle half of their sand.

Officiant: [Children's Names], come and join us.

Photos courtesy of Holly, Eric and their four children

This container (or containers) is here to show you, [Children's Names], that you're all in this together. Like colors of the rainbow, we're all different and special, valuable, and precious. Therefore, it's only fitting that you'll be able to tell just how very important you are to your parents. After all, marriage is about family and the close bonds of heart–how you feel–the kinds of things you think about, and the way you show up for each other, like enjoying what's going on when it's happening, right?

Your parents want to show you how important you are, and that they love you very much.

Are you ready?

Officiant to the children: Go ahead and pick up your vase of sand and add it to your Mom and Dad's.

Children picks up her/his container and add his/her sand. Officiant then turns attention back to the couple.

Officiant: [Couple's Names] you may finish pouring your sand.

Couple pours the rest of their sand into the jar.

Officiant: And now seal the vessel as a reminder that nothing is more important nor more sacred than the bond that you share as husband, wife, and family. [Child's Names], do you see where your sand is? Just like that sand, you're in the center of your mom and dad's hearts, now and forever.

Everyone returns to their original place before the Officiant.

42 10 WAYS TO ADD A BIT OF DAZZLE TO THE SAND CEREMONY

The traditional Sand Ceremony can have a lot of meaning. Combining the sands represents how all influences of the couple's individual pasts come together as one great union. A unique pattern is created so that we can explain that this is where the past meets the present. The Sand Ceremony is many small grains, many small joys and influences coming together to create great happiness. The ceremony is an exclamation point on what's being revealed.

Additionally, you can add after they've poured their sand at the same time, it's symbolic of them always going through life together. When the couple pours sand into vases separately it can show there's an ebb and flow in a normal relationship.

Dazzle #1 – the DIY'er
Color your own sand and add the different colors on the bottom before the ceremony to represent immediate family members.

How to color sand:
Step 1   Get some light-colored sand.
Step 2   Divide the sand into plastic zippered bags.
Step 3   Add a few drops of food coloring into each bag. Close the bags tightly, then shake and squeeze them to mix the sand.
Step 4   Transfer the sand to baking sheets.
Step 5   Allow the sand to dry overnight.
Step 6   Use your sand!

Dazzle #2 – the Parents
Choose two different colors of sand as a bottom layer to represent their parents' love. Either color can also represent the spiritual foundation of the marriage. Parents have the option of participating in the ceremony or the officiant can include this in her/his remarks.

Dazzle #3 – The Attendants

Supplies

Shallow bowl that can't be broken

Unique objects, in greater number than there are attendants so that everyone has a choice

This Dazzle can be used no matter how many attendants there are in the wedding party. The attendants each choose a gem, stone, bead, or another small item from a shallow bowl that's passed among them (started by the Besties) as the first step in the Sand Ceremony.

The couple pours either half their sand or all of it. Then the attendants file by and add their piece to the top of the sand. If the couple pours half their sand, after their attendants file by, they pour their remaining sand on top of objects.

Script

Officiant: The people who stand here with you today have greatly influenced your life. Your life has changed their life as well.

You've cried on each other's shoulders, cheered your favorite teams on, taken walks down dirt roads and city streets as you shared your troubles and joys, adopted dogs and cats, and welcomed children into your lives together.

Because they are such an integral part of your life, they are now invited to place an object that represents them into your Sand Ceremony vessel. This will be a reminder of your connection yesterday, today and in your tomorrows.

Objects are placed inside the vessel.

The couple can also give the jar a good shake to further symbolize how friends and family are part of the blending of family and friends.

Couple finishes pouring sand or places a lid on top of the vessel if applicable.

Ceremony proceeds.

Dazzle #4 – Time Factor

In this Dazzle, the central vessel is open at the top. The hourglass will actually do the combining of the colors into a unique pattern.

Supplies

An empty hourglass and base

Script

Officiant: [Couple's Names] are pouring their sand into the open top of this hourglass. The hourglass mixes their sand which represents how time has come together to bring them to their wedding day, and time will bring them closer as the days and years unfold.

Every time they turn the hourglass, it represents a new stage in their relationship. When they need to take a break in times of struggle, they can turn the hourglass and let the sand run out before continuing their discussion.

Likewise, in times of celebration, they can turn the hourglass to signify the start of good times coming.

The couple pours their sand into the hourglass. The top is put on the glass.

Ceremony proceeds.

Dazzle #5 – Spice of Life

Add dried herbs to the sand.

Different herbs have different meanings which can be detailed in your script. See the Herb Ceremony for their meaning. Use the Herb Ceremony script to include the meaning of the herbs as an added depth to the Sand Ceremony.

Dazzle #6 – Garden Grown

Have the couple choose if they're going to pour their combined sand into a special outdoor garden. Or they can mix their sand with soil that's at the base of a new tree they'll plant.

Supplies

A clear bag or a small sack (do not resort to a baggie) with a clear window in it if possible
2 small vessels that contain the couple's individual sand

Add the following text to the traditional text of the Sand Ceremony:

Script

Officiant: [Couple's Names] are putting their sand into this sack which so that when they return home, they'll use it to plant a special garden (or at the base of a new tree).

Couple pours their sand into the bag.

Officiant: Now their combined love will grow by giving life to the earth, the plants, and flowers.

Ceremony proceeds.

Dazzle #7 — Friends

Sometimes the couple asks the DJ or musicians to play background music while they pour their sand into the central vase. In this Dazzle, they ask a friend to read a poem while they combine their sand. It's great if the friend has written a pre-approved poem especially for the couple. If the couple likes this idea, and they don't have a poem already chosen, curate some selections for the friend from your own library. Or the couple might like the following:

Hand in Hand

by ShoeBowl, Author

Laying underneath the stars
On a warm silent night.
Your arms are wrapped around me,
And everything feels right.
You kiss me sweet and softly,
I feel your warm gentle touch,
You help me feel protected
Under the sweet night sky rush.

My world before me is perfect.
There's nowhere else I want to be,
Let's take a walk, my only love
Hand in hand, you and me.

Dazzle #8 – Goal of Growth

This Dazzle is about the couple helping each other accomplish their goals. To use this version, the couple can write their goals in a letter that can lay on top of the terrarium or is placed underneath. Then the couple can review the goals they've set monthly or whatever time frame they choose.

Supplies
Terrarium jar
Succulents that can grow in sand
Letter with the couple's goals
Same colored soil but may be combined with little bits of mica or crystals for sparkle

Script
Officiant: Not only will [Couple's Names] combined sand symbolize the foundation of a new and unique relationship but it will sustain life, even in situations like this small terrarium that they are going to fill first with sand. Nothing seems to be able to grow in sand, does it? But we're going to be pleasantly surprised in time.

Officiant sets up the meaning of the sand per the traditional Sand Ceremony script. Then, s/he directs the couple to take their vials of sand and combine their colors.

Couple pours their sand into the terrarium jar.

Officiant: Now they are going to plant these beautiful succulents on top of the sand. Each succulent represents a goal in their relationship.

Couple plants the succulents and then covers the terrarium with the proper lid or for the occasion places the letter with their goals in it on top.

Double Dazzle
The officiant asks the couple can state what their goals are.

The 9th Dazzle—Framing the Future

With this fun twist, the Sand Ceremony can be a projection of a vision for the future. Many options exist for the style of frame and having something inscribed or sand-blasted onto the glass.

Supplies

Frame with glass insert with favorite text etched onto it

See Link Directory for the following:

Available on Etsy: Unity Sand Frames

Set Up

With the couple, the officiant determines three or four words that describe a few goals the couple has for their relationship, including a goal they may have personally. These words can be sand-blasted or calligraphy used to write onto the frame's glass. OR small stones can have the words carved or written on them.

#10 Vision of Future Dazzle

Script

Officiant: A picture speaks a thousand words. Our couple is at the beginning of an adventure that will take them into the future. Their life together is going to be a unique mixture of ups and downs, tragedies, and celebrations.

Optional: As [Couple's Names] pour their individual sand into the frame, it represents a unique combination of influences. These experiences that have brought them to their wedding day now combine to show what's important to them.

Optional: These two have a vision for their future. And the words they're about to speak will be the internal frame for their future, the goals for their marriage. They are (examples: Devotion. Commitment. Fun. Support. Challenge to be my best.)

Sands are poured. Frame is closed.

Officiant: Congratulations on the beautiful future you have ahead of you. You have the strength and imagination to carry you through whatever may come, whenever it comes.

Couple returns to their place before the officiant. Ceremony proceeds.

"Many people lose small joys in the hope

for the big happiness." Pearl S. Buck

43 RITE OF THE SEVEN STEPS

This is my interpretation of the Cherokee Rite of the Seven Steps. In virtually every culture, the number seven is prominent. For example, the Bible refers to the seven days of creation, seven days of the week, the seven hills of Rome, seven enunciators of divine revelation in Islamic knowledge and many more. Broadly, the number seven is attributed with a mystical power which generally depicts perfection and completeness. The number seven is also associated with intuition, mysticism, inner wisdom, and a deep inward knowing.

For more information on the widespread use of the number seven check out Wikipedia's Symbolism of the Number Seven at Links Directory.

Supplies
Stakes option for vows being available at each step
Stake supplier see Link Directory

Set up
Fire pit: If there's a fire pit where a fire can be safely lit, the steps are taken around the fire pit. You can use lanterns as a substitute for the fire pit, but if the pit is small, or the lanterns are undersized, use the straight-line option.

Straight Line: In general, it's better for the couple to proceed in a straight line. Have the couple step to the back and move towards the middle of the main aisle and toward you. A bonus that comes with this ritual is guests can hear the couple speak their vows even more clearly.

Printed Copies: Print the following script twice on nice paper so the couple can hold it in their hands and follow along. See Dazzle for an alternative.

Caveat: This rite needs the couple's vows to contain 7 sentences or you can break up or combine their vows into seven phrases. You can make longer or shorter breaks they can repeat together with any vows. For the sake of example, the traditional vows are divided this way which creates seven steps:

Partner 1, I take you Partner 2 as my lawfully wedded wife/husband, // to have and to hold // from this day forward, // for better, for worse, // for richer, for poorer, // in sickness and in health // for as long as we both shall live.

The Officiant states the meaning of the first step, and the couple can either repeat their vow together, or one repeats the vow, then the other, and together they take a step forward. Repeat with the meaning of the second step, and so on.

Script

Step 1
Officiant: The first step in this rite establishes that this is a new day. You are willing to join your hearts fully as one. If you agree, speak your first vow.
Couple: Partner1, I take you Partner2 as my lawfully, wonderfully created wife/husband.
They take one step together.

Step 2
Officiant: You awaken to this relationship being unlike any other, totally new. If you agree, speak your second vow.
Couple: To have and to hold They take one step together.

Step 3
Officiant: You have faith in each other that you'll have each other's best interests in mind day after day, year after year. If you agree, speak your third vow.
Couple: From this day forward.
They take one step together.

Step 4
Officiant: You will be using your imagination to envision a wonderful life together. If you agree, speak your fourth vow.
Couple: For better, for worse.

They take one step together.

Step 5
Officiant: You're agreeing that you'll weather any storm and celebrate every gift of life more fully together. If you are in agreement, speak your fifth vow.
Couple: In sickness and in health.
They take one step together.

Step 6
Officiant: You resolve as you grow together love will always become more than it was yesterday. If you agree, speak your sixth vow.
Couple: For as long as we both shall live.
They take one step together.

Step 7
Officiant: Though you know these are solemn vows, you won't take yourself too seriously, and you will fulfill these vows every day to the best of your ability. If you agree, speak your seventh vow.
Couple: We do!

Couple returns to the altar with the Officiant and exchange their rings.

A Bit of Dazzle
Set out seven stations that each hold the next line of their vows rather than carrying a script around, or the officiant leads them to repeat after her/him. Stands can be similar to the small metal stakes that hold jars and flowers that often decorate the end of the aisles at a wedding ceremony. A jar hanging from the stakes holds the vows for that step.

Carrie and Jason Smith at their Rite of the Seven Steps Ceremony

44 STEFANA CROWNS

Perhaps you remember the wedding ceremony from the 2002 movie, *My Big Fat Greek Wedding.*

Here's a way to make a portion of a Greek wedding ceremony into your contemporary couple's special celebration.

This is a contemporary version of a very rich and symbolic Greek wedding tradition. Use it in part or as a whole for a couple that loves the idea of re-imagining tradition.

Historical Perspective

The tradition of the priest or officiant placing a delicate, white crown on top of the couple's head was said to originate in the 11th century and is still one of the most important traditional Greek wedding traditions. Greek wedding ceremonies feature an elaborate ritual with the crowns. A key person, the wedding sponsor, called the Koumbaros, is essential to this ceremony. While the Koumbaros is typically the Best Man, anyone who holds a special place in the heart of the couple is the perfect choice for this role.

Resources

For Crowns, and to view a traditional version of the Stefana Crowns ceremony, see the Link Directory.

Process

At the onset, a prayer is said or a set of affirmations are led by the officiant which the couple can repeat after the officiant.

Next is the Betrothal Ceremony where the wedding rings are blessed and exchanged.

The officiant then places crowns on each of their heads. The Koumbaros intertwines the crowns three times while over the couple's heads to symbolize the couple's individual lives are being given to each other in unity.

Lastly, the couple drinks wine from the Common Cup in remembrance of the miracle of their love. At the end of the ceremony, the officiant removes the Stefana crowns and prays for the couple's marriage.

Set Up

There are two main parts of the Greek wedding service, the Betrothal Ceremony, and the Marriage Service. Within the Marriage Service, there are four main sections. Before these rituals take place, prayer or affirmations are appropriate, and there are several suggestions in the script.

The four sections of the Marriage Service are the
> 1. Crowning Ritual, the prominent element of this ceremony includes the Betrothal Ceremony and Marriage Service
> 2. Sacrament of the Common Cup
> 3. Ceremonial Walk
> 4. Removing the Stefana Crowns

Supplies

Table
Wedding Rings
Stefana crowns with white ribbon joining them together
Cup from which to drink the wine

Betrothal Ceremony

This can be a very complicated service to do. But it's full of symbolism and can be quite a spiritual process.

In Greek Ceremonies, the rings are exchanged first. The rings are blessed and the symbolism explained. As a traditional blessing, the officiant may pass her or his hand over the rings as the couple repeats each of the following statements after the Officiant.

Officiant: In my hands are the rings that [Couple's Names] have chosen to represent their commitment to love one another for a lifetime.

These rings are blessed by the Heart of God which is the essence of the love you have found. Please repeat after me:

Couple: The Divine is the Source of our Love for each other.

These rings are blessed by the attraction you felt for each other, inspired by the Love that is greater than you now know calling you into a fuller expression of love.

Divine Love is calling you to become the full expression of all that Love can be.

Your rings are made of precious metals and have beautiful shine, angles, and jewels which represents the expression of love that will carry you through whatever life may bring you as long as you remain true to your commitment to know love.

Couple: We remain true to our commitment to know love for as long as we both shall live.

Officiant: Now the Koumbaras will exchange the rings over and under your fingers three times, symbolic of Divine Love, the couple's journey to know the depths of love, and [Couple's Names] commitment to know love for the rest of their lives together.

The Koumbaras passes the rings over and under the same fingers on the couple's joined hands three times. Then s/he gives the couple the rings and they place their rings on the fourth finger on each other's left hand.

The Marriage Service

Officiant prayer: Thank you, Loving Spirit for [Couple's Name] tenderness of heart and touch and spiritual bond. We declare this marriage service opens their hearts and minds to the wonder of who they are as individuals and as a couple.

The Crowning

Officiant: You have been created in the image and likeness of God. You are in essence part of the royal family of the Divine and have the pleasure, the right, and responsibility to create wisely, and to bring to bear a relationship that not only blesses the two of you but makes you a light in the world.

The Stefana crowns are symbolic of your royal heritage, that you are the king and queen of your life.

Officiant holds the crowns in her/his hands, emphasizing the white ribbon which symbolizes the unity that joins them as one.

Officiant: God's Love has made you and fills your minds with wisdom so your love carries the power of insight and good judgment. I place these crowns on your heads to show that you are ready to be channels for the knowledge of the Divine to flow to and through you in this marriage. The white ribbon joins you together so you remember your unity, to always talk things through, be vulnerable, and caring of one another's thoughts, feelings, goals, and ideas.

Koumbaras exchanges the crowns three times between the two to represent the divine instruction to be unified in the purpose.

Optional
Koumbaras: May you be unified in purpose, in body (exchange crown first time), mind, (exchange crown second time), and soul (exchange crown third time.)

The Common Cup
Officiant: We believe that all things are possible through the love of God which is God's gift to you as members of the royal family.

Jesus changed water into wine at the wedding ceremony in Cana. Remember this and the power given to you to be lights in the world. Know that your love and the actions you take together reveal the miracle of love's power in your love for each other is symbolized by drinking wine.

Officiant: Will you act as one?
Couple: Yes. We will act as one.
They drink from the cup once.

Officiant: Will you allow the miracles of God to work through you for others as well as for yourselves?
Couple: Yes. We allow the miracles of God to work through us.
Couple drinks from the cup a second time.

Officiant: Will you celebrate your marriage as a gift from God?
Couple: Yes, we celebrate our marriage as a gift from the Divine.
Couple drinks from the cup a third time.

The Ceremonial Walk
The officiant next leads the couple who are still wearing their Stefana crowns three times around the altar on their first walk as a married couple. Walking behind them is their Koumbara who makes sure the crowns stay

on their heads. If the couple is very religious they can kiss the Bible three times, or any other sacred text they choose.

Removing the Crowns

Once the walk around the altar table has ended, the officiant can bless the couple a final time and then remove the crowns.

Officiant: [Couple's Names], may you live a long, healthy, prosperous, and happy life together, filled with miracles that will amaze you when you least expect it. Let the love you know grow ever more delightful and be a source of peace in the midst of life's trials and joys. Remember that wherever you go, whatever you do, love is always with you, and is the healer, the director, the truth of who you are.

Crowns are removed. Officiant officially pronounces the couple married and introduces them to guests.

As the couple exits, rice is thrown at them to symbolize health, fertility, wealth, and longevity in their life together.

Photo by permission, Marina Vazura on Etsy.com

45 ON LOVE

Our couples often select a favorite reading that share their sentiments about the power of the love they're committing to. Here's a reading my couples' have appreciated year after year. It's written by the amazing Bob Marley.

Only once in your life, I truly believe, you find someone who can completely turn your world around.

You tell them things that you've never shared with another soul and they absorb everything you say, and actually want to hear more.

You share hopes for the future, dreams that will never come true, goals that were never achieved and the many disappointments life has thrown at you.

When something wonderful happens, you can't wait to tell them about it, knowing they will share in your excitement.

They are not embarrassed to cry with you when you are hurting or laugh with you when you make a fool of yourself.

Never do they hurt your feelings or make you feel like you are not good enough, but rather they build you up and show you the things about yourself that make you special and even beautiful.

There is never any pressure, jealousy, competition, but only a quiet calmness when they are around.

You can be yourself and not worry about what they will think of you because they love you for who you are.

The things that seem insignificant to most people such as a note, song, or walk, become invaluable treasures kept safe in your heart to cherish forever.

Memories of your childhood come back and are so clear and vivid it's like being young again.

Colors seem brighter and more brilliant. Laughter seems part of daily life where before it was infrequent or didn't exist at all. A phone call or two during the day helps to get you through a long day's work and always brings a smile to your face.

In their presence, there's no need for continuous conversation, but you find yourself quite content in just having them nearby.

Things that never interested you before become fascinating because you know they are important to this person who is so special to you.

You think of this person on every occasion and in everything you do. Simple things bring them to mind like a pale blue sky, gentle wind or even a storm cloud on the horizon.

You open your heart knowing that there's a chance it may be broken one day and in opening your heart, you experience a love and joy that you never dreamed possible.

You find that being vulnerable is the only way to allow your heart to feel true pleasure that's so real it scares you. You find strength in knowing you have a true friend and possibly a soul mate who will remain loyal to the end.

Life seems completely different, exciting, and worthwhile. Your only hope and security is in knowing that they are a part of your life.

Bob Marley

Photo of pearls by Tiffany Anthony on Unsplash

46 STRINGING THE PEARLS

Everyone, and certainly a couple, appreciates being acknowledged by their friends. A compliment can go a long way to soften a nervous moment. Almost every person who stands in front of others and is the center of attention, like in a wedding ceremony, experiences uneasiness.

Many officiants also experience uneasiness. But it can be tempered once we're appreciated after the wedding we've conducted is over. When we're thanked for our work, any worry disappears. One of my favorite things to do is turn the compliment around by saying, "It's so kind of you to say that."

I admit it, let's all admit that compliments and appreciation are helpful and welcome regardless of the situation.

Appreciation is a pat on the back with words. They confirm that a good job has been done. Another example of the power of appreciation is when I led workshops as a minister where, at the end of the event, the participants debrief using a simple technique called, "Stringing the Pearls." Participants get into a circle and give feedback about their experience in the seminar. It's a good way to learn what worked and what didn't.

A few years ago, I was the designated officiant for a winter wedding giveaway contest that 18 wedding professionals collaborated on in my area. The winners received $35,000 worth of services. The participation was crazy good. Every one of our social media accounts blew up for almost a month.

Our winning couple was fairly traditional but I kept thinking about

Stringing the Pearls. I enjoy creating ceremonies, and I decided to create something unique for this couple that could also bolster their confidence both as a couple and as individuals.

Plus, interactive ceremonies can be very fun to do.

This simple easy special ceremony has been well-received. Use this ceremony when there are at least three attendants. When the MOH and BM agree to participate, I email them the directions below as well as the YouTube snippet video from the first time I did this ceremony included below. I suggest an officiant add Stringing the Pearls early in the main ceremony because some people are nervous about even saying one word in front of people.

BTW Stringing the Pearls is a surprise for the couple. When you explain the package to a potential couple in your discovery meeting tell them a surprise is included. For some, this may become an incentive to hire you in order to find out what that surprise is!

This ceremony is such a great way for the people chosen by the wedding pair to be supportive of the couple, to sum up why they're friends as they transition from being single to becoming a married couple.

See the winter wedding giveaway ceremony: Stringing the Pearls video

Process

The Maid/Matron of Honor and the Best Man have to be enlisted. To come off without being cheesy it's best to have three or more attendants on each side.

1. Ask your couple for their Maid/Matron of Honor and Best Man's contact information either with the pretense of interviewing them for their thoughts about what a great couple they are, or you just want to get familiar with their circle of friends and family so your ceremony will be better.

2. When contacting the Maid / Matron of Honor and Best Man explain the concept of surprising the couple with praise and compliments about the couple's character at the start of the wedding.

3. If Maid/Matron of Honor and the Best Man are on board, ask them to get in touch with each member of the wedding party on their "side" and explain the "Stringing the Pearls" process to them.

4. Each person is asked to determine a word or "pearl" of appreciation/admiration they have for the Partner1 or Partner2 they are standing with. Emphasize A WORD or you may get people saying more than is necessary.

5. For this to go smoothly, each person needs to speak their word without hesitation. It's not difficult and is a touching and meaningful surprise to the couple to be honored this way in front of all their guests.

6. Early in the ceremony after the presentation and welcoming words have been given, choose the best time to set the ceremony in motion.

Optional

The following can be forwarded by the Maid/Matron of Honor and Best Man to each attendant in the wedding party so each one of them has the same directions.

Partner1's attendants speak their words first, working from the end towards the Maid / Matron of Honor. Then over to the person at the end on the Partner2's side, working inward to the Best Man.

Script

Officiant: [Couple's Names], you are two people who are highly regarded and loved. And your friends and family have some pearls of appreciation they want to say about the kind of person you are…

Attendants share their words. "____, _____, _____, _____, _____, _____, _____, _____."

Officiant: Do you see how much your friends and family appreciate you? You have made the world a better place because of your love not only for each other but for your friends and family also. We begin your ceremony today with a lot of love for the wonderful people you are. Optional: Are you ready to continue?

Ceremony proceeds.

Guidelines for the Attendants

Stringing the Pearls Question: What ONE WORD would you use to describe the character or quality of your friend/family member?

1. If you're not sober, please don't participate.
2. Limit what you say to ONE WORD/one thought. Please don't let yourself get carried away which may be a double challenge if you've been drinking too much. This is not the time to make a big speech. Save the speech for the reception.
3. Everyone say their word immediately after the person they follow. When it's your turn to share your word, go for it.
4. You MUST have fun doing this. (Most important guideline of all).

A Bit of Dazzle

Ask the Maid/Matron of Honor and Best Man to record the words each attendant plan to share so they can be given to the couple in a written copy of the ceremony you give your couple afterward.

47 TASTING THE FOUR ELEMENTS

Tasting of the four elements is a representation of how a marriage can have its ups and downs and how the couple who vows to love "for better or worse, for richer or poorer, and in sickness and health" will be challenged and rewarded over time. Just like it's great to watch the partners see each other for the first time walking up the aisle, it can also be fun to see the looks on the couple's faces when they test the different tastes.

Supplies
Lemon juice or a lemon cut in a lemon wedge
Vinegar or vinegar and water
Cayenne Pepper or jalapeno
Honey or jam Small bowls or glass
Small spoon
Table

Process
Place the four elements in small bowls or glasses for tasting prior to the actual ceremony.

Script
Officiant: It's easy to say I love you but it's not always so easy to love each other day after day, year after year.

Most couples believe from the start of their marriage that they can avoid the conflicts and problems that "other couples do because our love for each other is different."

[Couple's Names] are well aware of the up and down nature of relationships and are going to participate in the Tasting of the Four Elements ceremony today. This ceremony reminds them of the reality of "in sickness AND in health, for better OR for worse, for the times they'll be pinching pennies AND when they're rolling in cash." Yes, [Couple's Names], know about the ups and downs love goes through because it's already happened in their relationship.

Is this true?

Couple: Yes!!

Officiant: What's bitter and sour, spicy and sweet are normal experiences in a healthy relationship. They aren't to be avoided, but expected and loved through. These emotions and experiences are not the greatest expression of love but can certainly deepen your love when you let the taste of sourness, bitterness, spiciness, and sweetness wear away.

In a moment, you're going to exchange your vows and rings and make important pledges that will carry you through the thick and thin that love goes through. Tasting the four elements represents your willingness to hold as sacred the vows you are about to make no matter what happens in your lives together.

Behind the officiant is a table with the glasses or small bowls filled with the element.

Officiant: Tasting the Sour (Lemon) represents the individual sacrifice that each person has to make within the marriage to be as one, which may cause sour feelings.

Couple dips their finger in the lemon juice OR they squeeze a bit of lemon juice into each other's mouth (bridal gown protected) and taste the sour.

Officiant: Bitterness may develop within the relationship when one gives more than the other. Be mindful that a successful relationship asks each person to give 100% of him or herself, not 50% / 50%.

Couple dip their fingers in the vinegar and tastes it.

Officiant: Oh how most of us dislike arguing. But every relationship has its moments of heated disagreements and this is true for [Couple's Names]. Taste now from the cup of heat (cayenne pepper).

Officiant takes the small spoon and gets a pinch of pepper from the bowl, and drops it into the outstretched hand of each person. The couple tastes it.

Officiant: But no relationship must ever be all bitter and sour. Spice can be counterbalanced with sweet. Marriage is sweet. It's openness of heart, mind, and touch. The sweet is unconditional Love.

Officiant holds out the small dish of honey to the couple. Couple dips their finger in the honey and tastes it.

Officiant: By tasting all these elements, [Couple's Names] have shown they can "weather the storm" of the sour, bitter, and heat of their marriage and remain in love (the sweetness).

A Bit of Dazzle
After the couple taste the element, they kiss each other's cheek.

Dazzle Alternatives to the bare element
Bitter: Bite into a lemon square without sugar
Sour: Drink water and vinegar
Heat: Feed each other a jalapeno instead of cayenne
Sweet: Have a cracker with honey on it or a fruit jam.

48 TREE PLANTING

So many couples these days are concerned about and are invested in saving the environment. Planting a tree is a way to remind a couple of their wedding day, and take an important environmental action.

Trees also have a symbolic meaning based on the type of tree they choose. The Tree Ceremony emphasizes their growth as a couple and the need to tend to their relationship as they would a tree. Weaving the specific meaning into a couple's ceremony makes this expression of commitment all the more special.

Consideration
Some couples may be concerned about handling dirt when they're so dressed up. An option for them is to water the tree instead.

Supplies
Tree in a pot
Table to set tree on
2 bags or jars of soil
Optional: 2 small watering cans

Script
[Couple's Names] are now going to take part in a Tree Planting Ceremony, to symbolize the roots of their relationship, and the continued growth of their love as they become each other's family today.

Love is the essence of human experience and emotion. It is at the root of everything we do. Love enriches our experience, and fills our lives with meaning. It gives us a firm base from which to grow, to learn, and change.

[Couple's Names] have chosen *Name of tree* which represent *add symbolic meaning.*

Let your relationship and your love for each other be like this tree you plant/water today. Let it grow tall and strong. Let it stand strong during the harsh winds, rains, and storms, and come through unscathed. Like a tree, your marriage must be resilient. It must weather the challenges of daily life and the passage of time. Just like the tree you are planting, marriage requires constant nurturing and nourishment.

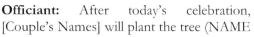

Invite the couple to come to their new tree. They place the dirt or water around the base of the tree.

Officiant: After today's celebration, [Couple's Names] will plant the tree (NAME LOCATION) to symbolize putting down roots, longevity and strength in their marriage.

May you dig down deep into the love all around you, and enjoy the beauty and function of your beautiful tree!

Couple return to their place and the ceremony proceeds.

Symbolic meaning of specific trees
NOTE: *Check that a species you may be interested in is not invasive in your area.*

Birch. Because of their year-round beauty, birch trees symbolize hope and new beginnings. Birch can also mean protection, purification, and love.

Box Elder. Abundance.

Cherry. Good fortune and luck when they bloom, but can also be a reminder that life is short and that people should live every day to the fullest. Cherry trees can also mean love, adoration, and romance.

Dogwood. Durability, Loyalty, safety, kindness, fertility, stability, determination, wishes, and protection. In Native American culture, dogwood trees symbolize good luck. While their flowers appear gentle and small, they're actually strong enough to endure harsh conditions, hence durability.

Elm. Inner strength and love. Because of the way the Dutch Elm disease wiped out our elms, Mountain Elms aren't prey to the disease.

Fir. Springtime, fortitude, and immortality.

Japanese Maple. Grace, great blessing, serenity of the elements, and peaceful retreat.

Maple. Balance, offering, practical magic, promise, longevity, generosity, and intelligence. Maple trees have the ability to adapt to many different soil types and climates. Because some maples produce maple syrup (sugar, black, red and silver maple) they can also represent abundance and success.

Pine. Endurance. Because it's an evergreen, this amazing tree never loses it leaves even in the winter when other trees do, hence no matter happens, it is full of life.

Oak. These trees are a symbol of courage and power, strength and resilience. Oak wilt has also wiped out a huge number of oaks in the United States, so this may not be a good tree to plant at this time.

Poplars. Abundance, independence, and resilience.

Redwood. Eternity and the ability to withstand conflict and tragedy, and bask in goodness.

Willow. Flexibility, inner wisdom, dreams, harmony, and freedom.

A Bit of Dazzle

Throughout the world there are organizations that plant a tree in someone's name and you can donate to one of these organizations for your couple. The median cost to plant a tree is $20.

One of the actions I recommend is for an officiant to donate to a non-profit organization they feel makes the world a better place in honor of their couple.

Another option is set aside $5 or $10/couple who uses the Tree Planting Ceremony. At the end of the wedding season, you'll have a bigger group donation to give your chosen group. In honor of the donation you make, create an acknowledgement certificate which you can send or email to the couple. Some organizations may provide a certificate so be sure to ask them if this is a possibility.

One of the groups who will plant a tree is OneTreePlanted.org. Or do a search for non-profit tree planters.

Another Bit of Dazzle is to sponsor a student who wants to become a Master Gardener. Most community colleges and agricultural departments have a program where you can be a sponsor.

Yet another option is to volunteer for an environmental group in honor of your couple(s).

Last but not least, at the base of the tree in its final planting space place a letter written by the couple that outlines their hopes and dreams for their relationship. This letter can be referenced at the end of the ceremony.

Photo of tree seedling, page 187, Anna Shvets on Pexels.com.

Photo, Arthouse Photos, pexels.com

49 TRUCE BELLS

The Bell of Truce originates from west Ireland peasant traditions, believed to be derived from St. Patrick's Bell of Will. The bell represents spiritual leadership and the call to peace.

Historical Perspective

According to legend, whenever Saint Patrick had set up a new Christian community or parish somewhere in Ireland, he would choose one of his disciples to lead it after he'd departed. He'd present the new leader with a bell to call the parishioners to prayer, and to use during their religious ceremonies. Apparently in Connaught alone he had bestowed over fifty bells, and at one point had as many as three smiths among his followers who were employed full-time to make bells. The bells he and his disciples used were small, handheld objects, made from iron and formed into a quadrangle with rounded corners.

Process

The newly married couple is asked to give the Bell of Truce a good hardy ring at the same time while thinking lovely thoughts of each other and, most importantly, of their future together. This can be done before or after they share their vows but I prefer that they ring the bell after they share their vows. Another option is ringing the Truce Bells after a reading like On Marriage by Kahlil Gibran, or From Letters to a Young Poet by Rainer Maria Rilke. After the ceremony, the couple can display the bell in a prominent location in their home.

When that inevitable disagreement arises, one or both members of the couple may ring the bell, calling a truce to the discord without admitting fault. Upon hearing the lovely tone of the bell, the couple will be reminded of their wedding vows. The resulting fond and happy memories of that day are intended to bring peace to the home and restore a proper balance to the relationship.

Supplies

Truce Bell for the couple
Optional: Small bells for guests
See Link Directory for resources to purchase bells

Script

Officiant: Now that [Couple's Names] have shared their vows and committed their hearts to one another, they want us to join them in the ringing of the Truce Bells.

Addressed to the guests: We all know what it means to call a truce, yes?

Answer: Yes!!

While we are all gathered here to witness the vows and the best intentions [Couple's Names] share, there may come times in the future when this couple has their differences. And they may be beyond our reach in space and time. But [Couple's Names] are never beyond the reach of our blessings and prayers, for there's no distance in Spirit.

They are going to ring this bell, and ring the Truce Bell with all their hearts.

As they do, please send your best wishes into the bell. Let your thoughts and prayers include reminding them that in their times of conflict and separation, that they call out for the great Love that brought them together to remind them of their wedding vows, and how they are more together than alone.

Fill the ringing of the bell with the knowledge that when they come back to center to work through their differences in honor of their vows, the solution will become clear. To indeed, call a truce so that from a place of peace, they discover their common purpose once again.

Officiant to the couple: As you ring the Truce Bell, think only of how much you mean to each other, and let the sound be filled with your love for each other.

Optional: Guests, when they ring their bell, ring the bell you received when you entered this space, with [Couple's Names].

Ring that bell! *Bell is rung.*

Officiant: The Truce Bell doesn't mean you should never disagree. It may mean you'll be asked to put aside your differences, but never give up on your love and what brought you together.

Therefore, if and when you have an argument, ring the Truce Bell. When you hear the tone of the bell, may you be reminded of your wedding vows. Remember fond and happy memories of today so there's peace in your home and balance is restored to the relationship.

Ceremony proceeds.

A Bit of Dazzle

Most craft stores sell small bells, the kind that you can hang on a door pull or use to make an ornament. Purchase enough of these small bells to accommodate your guests. To decorate, add a ribbon or cord to the bell top. Hand the finished bell to each guest so when the couple ring their Truce Bell, guests can ring their mini-bell with them.

50 UNITY REACTION

For those who aren't interested in an alcohol-based Wine Box, Bourbon Unity or Mead ceremony, the Unity Reaction Ceremony is a fun alternative (with some cautions). This ceremony still makes a statement that the couple's commitment changes both partners. All they bring to their relationship helps them to change, to grow and unfold into better people.

Supplies
Sodium Hydroxide (lye)
Disappearing ink
White Vinegar
Two small jars
One larger central jar
Table

Resources
For inks, sodium hydroxide, a photo of the ceremony, and precautions, see the Link Directory.
Caution: When the couple experiments as explained below, use a rubber apron, rubber gloves, and safety glasses.

Directions
To make the liquid in the individual jars blue, combine disappearing ink and sodium hydroxide. You'll have to experiment with amounts in order to get the ink to stay blue/purple. But the more lye you add, the more vinegar you'll need to add to get the ink to change to clear liquid.

Half fill the central unity jar with white vinegar, leaving room for the blue liquid to be poured in the jar without spilling over.

Script

Officiant: Love changes us. It's not uncommon that to the one in love colors look brighter, food tastes better, the air smells fresher. Everything changes for the better when we are in love.

[Couple's Names] you have exchanged your vows and rings to declare the promises you're committed to. Keeping these commitments will undoubtedly change you and take you on a journey full of adventures that can be all you hoped for and more.

Indeed, [Couple's Names] you are bringing together all the best, worst, bitter, and sweet experiences that you've been through. There's water under the bridge; water to quench your thirst, water to cleanse your soul, and lift your spirits.

By committing to each other, you're stating that together your lives will be transformed through good times and bad, whether you're rolling in cash or pinching pennies, or you are healthy or are under the weather.

The two jars of water symbolize the true, blue nature of the lives you've lived before your marriage. By combining the waters, you are confirming your eagerness to be changed and cleansed and uplifted.

You may now pour the blue liquid into the unity jar. Let's see what happens!

Couple pours the water into the unity jar. (Water becomes clear.)

Officiant: And so the transformation begins! May your journey into marriage year after year show you the depths and heights of the love you're committing to today.

A Bit of Dazzle

Use an exceptionally large glass so that everyone can clearly see the color change. A bit of dry ice can be kept in a separate box below the changing water vase. The couple can release the cold "smoke" either before or after they've combined their water.

51 WALL OF LIGHTS

The Wall of Lights Ceremony creates a special atmosphere with a large amount of lights. It also increases the feeling of community and symbolizes the small light each guest contributes that together make a greater light. It's best done with a smaller group of people, although for more people, several walls of lights could safely accommodate more people. However, this will also increase the amount of time needed to complete the ceremony.

Consider these limitations before doing this ceremony if real candles are used:

~ Not suitable for a ceremony held outdoors, nor during the day

~ Real candles mean using extra care

~ Be mindful of weather conditions even if this is not performed outside

~ Not recommended for large groups of people

~ Insurance coverage that may be required

Option

Using battery-operated candles is probably the best way to go for safety's sake and ease of use. This ceremony will still be lovely and meaningful.

Supplies

Table or many candle holders (vary in height) for guests to set the lights on behind the altar

Candles, votive candles, or battery-operated candles for guests

Two tapers and one larger candle for the couple

Water to put out flames or a fire extinguisher

Candle snuffer

Floor covering to protect from dripping wax

Good quality wood stick matches

Photo of candles by Mike Labrum on Unsplash.com

Script

Officiant: Everyone who has been invited here today to witness [Couple's Names] commitment to each other, has influenced them. You have helped to make these two who they needed to be in order to find each other.

You are a light in their lives, now and always.

Your lights together help to light the journey ahead of them.

They will light two individual candles which represent the light they are to each other and to the world.

Then together they will light one candle that represents the blending of their light into one; for together, their light is brighter than one light alone.

[Couple's Names], your individual candles, represents your individual lives, your individual experiences, good times and bad, and the gifts you bring to your relationship.

Please light your individual candle.

Couple lights their candles and step back. Do not light the big unity candle.

[Couple's Names] your love for one another is a light in the world.

Officiant addressing the guests: I invite each of you here you to take a moment to consider something that can only be felt in the heart. But it is an important gift you can give today to [Couple's Names].

Please close your eyes. Go into your heart for a moment and identify a wish or prayer for [Couple's Names] future. What does your heart say will lead them to their greatest happiness?

There are no right or wrong wishes and prayers when we begin in our heart.

Take a moment to listen to what your heart wishes for [Couple's Names] future.

Pause for 30 seconds.

Officiant: Does everyone know what their wish is? Wanting general great happiness is also a wonderful gift of light.

One at a time by row, you're invited to create a Wall of Lights. Choose a candle and in the powerful presence of your heart, either silently or aloud, speak your wish for this couple as you light a candle for them.

Give a moment between rows so no one has to stand backed up in a line.

People file to the back of the altar to light their candle, return to their seat and then sit back down.
When everyone is seated:

Officiant: You can see the power and beauty of these lights together. [Couple's Names] see how the friendships you have formed will be with you not only from the past but as guiding lights in your future?

To the couple: With these lights behind you and with your individual lights, it's time for you to light the candle that represents all of your lights coming together as one.

You come together as lights celebrating this day, and taking the next steps into your mysterious future. But you will never be alone. The light is with you always.

Couple light their large unity candle.

Officiant: Such a beautiful sight to see all of the light of your friends and family together with yours, and to go forward into the future knowing the light is always with you wherever you go, whatever you do.

Proceed with the remainder of the ceremony.

Caution

Be sure to extinguish lit candles as soon as the ceremony is over or photos have been taken. Don't leave lit candles unattended.

A Bit of Dazzle

Instead of candles, pass out small sparklers. Light the sparklers from the center aisle outward. Check with the couple to see if there will be a lot of children. We don't want them burned or getting out of hand by waving around sparklers.

Photo by permission, Kachinahouse.com

52 WEDDING VASE

Background

The Wedding Vase is an ancient vessel used in traditional Native American wedding ceremonies. You've probably seen these vessels in art galleries and museums and perhaps wondered what they're for because they look so unique.

That's because these vessels have two spouts. One spout of the vessel is symbolic of the husband or Partner1; the other represents the wife or Partner2. The looped handle represents the oneness achieved within the marriage.

The space created within the loop represents the couple's own circle of life. For example, instead of grains of sand (the Sand Ceremony) representing all the different influences that have made each person who s/he is and how they are made one by the combining of the sands, the space within the loop represents the encompassing influence of the couple's love in the world.

Traditionally, before the ceremony, the parents give the young couple advice, and the wedding vase is filled with a special liquid. Traditionally it would be a nectar made by the medicine man, though many modern couples may choose to drink water or an herbal tea from the vase to represent the blending of their lives.

Resources
To purchase authentic Wedding Vases, visit Kachinahouse.com.

Script
Officiant: The Wedding Vase has two spouts. One spout represents the husband/Partner2; the other represents the wife/Partner1. The looped handle and rounded base represent the oneness that is achieved as the couple become more and more one within the marriage. The space created within the loop represents the power of the breath, the air contained within their bodies. This is our couple's own circle of life.

To begin, Partner2 offers Partner1 the vessel. Partner1 drinks from one spout.

Next, Partner1 turns the wedding vase clockwise.

Following, Partner2 drinks from the same side as did Partner1.

Officiant: Drinking from the same spout represents appreciating the strengths [Couple's Names] brings to this marriage.

Each person drinks from the opposite side of the wedding vase.

Officiant: Drinking from the same spout represents appreciating the strengths the Partner1/Partner 1 brings to this marriage.

To conclude the ceremony, the couple both drink from the wedding vase together.

Officiant: The rounded base and shared reservoir of the vase represent the new shared life the couple has committed to.

It's said that if the couple can manage this feat without spilling a drop they will always have a strong, cooperative relationship. The vase then becomes a cherished piece of remembrance in the household and great care is taken to make sure it is never damaged.

NOTE: If the couple spills the liquid, the officiant can always say something to the effect, "This is just the beginning of their life together and faith in each other and themselves will bring to life unexpected and welcomed strengths."

A Bit of Dazzle

Before the Wedding Vase ceremony begins acknowledge the elders who are present.

This second Dazzle is a bit more complicated. First a bit of history.

The common Native American greeting for guests was not "Hello" or "How are you doing?" or even "Good to see you." It was always "Have you eaten?" For many Native American Nations, there was no set meal time. Whenever one was hungry they dipped into the contemporary metal or original gourd or wooden containers and had something to eat. This was typically a stew of meat, or fish with vegetables or hominy. The stew was replenished by always replacing what had been taken. For example, if a piece of meat or fish was removed a piece of meat or fish was added. If stock was removed then water and other fillers or thickeners was added and so forth.

This practice was nicknamed The Eternal Cooking Meal. Not all couples will be interested in being fully immersed in Native American culture. So of course, check with the couple to see if they're interested in this kind of practice. If they are, arrange for the Eternal Cooking Meal with the couple's family or wedding planner.

53 WEDDING ZEN

In his book, *Best. Ceremony. Ever.* Christopher Shelley, Officiant, shares an element of his ceremonies called Wedding Zen.

Zen is an Eastern philosophy that's related to Buddhism, and is actually a branch of Secular Buddhism. Wedding Zen is about being called back to the present moment, or to be mindfulness of the instances they are in which is powerful and magical. Wedding Zen is an antidote to couples being distracted on their wedding day, ready for the party that's coming up next, so that they miss out on the preciousness of the new feel of the rings on their fingers, the odd and expected sounds around them. Chris created this part of his ceremony to encourage his couples to pay attention to what they're feeling and seeing and being.

In our wedding planning session, I ask my couples if they're open to this ceremony. Some are very Christian and might not want to include it. "I never announce, 'And now we're going to experience Wedding Zen,'" I explain. "I just invite you into the practice before I offer my final thoughts." One after the other has said, "Yes," regardless of their religious affiliation (if they even have one.) I'm happy to report -- every couple has loved this ceremony. I'm often told afterwards by a guest, "The centering at the end was a great touch."

Christopher is imaginative, funny and his book inspired me to lighten up the way I deliver my ceremonies. If you resonate with this ceremony, present it to one of your couples. Give it a try. Get Chris's book on Amazon. *Best. Ceremony. Ever.* See Link Directory.

Script

Take note of the temperature in the air and the sounds around you.

Feel what it's like to be here, surrounded by those who have come from near and far to be with you, because they love you and only want the best for you.

Drink in the sight, sound and feel of the person standing here with you whom you love more than anyone else. Notice the feeling of each other's hands, and the weight of the rings on your fingers.

And then one more thing--think back to the very first moment you met. Back when it all started, and how that moment has led you here today.

Proceed with the ceremony.

A Bit of Dazzle

Direct the couple to look out at their guests in paragraph two and take in the smiling, supportive faces of all their friends and family. Or for the last line, ask the couple to tell the story of how they met. Couples often laugh at this last suggestion, so it could be fun to find out what made them chuckle. At this point, most couples are ready to kiss and move on.

Encourage the couple to commit to a time during their celebration when one of them takes the other aside to reconnect and note what they're feeling inside.

For example, help each other notice how they're doing, (they love seeing grandma dancing, or all that glass clanging to insist they kiss, or to admit how that person who keeps pulling them over to talk with them is stressful) who they've talked to, and ask if they need anything. It's a great time for a private hug. Give themselves one minute, which they time, to just stand with each other and neither of them say nor do anything.

Take a deep breath, become present again to each other and then return to the celebration.

54 A FATHER'S WINE

My officiant career began in Atlanta, Georgia in 1990.

Ever since I started to conduct weddings I rarely stayed for the reception, because I quickly learned that few people knew what to do with me (honored person or ordinary vendor status). The couple have dozens of people to connect with them and they don't need one more. The festivities get along just fine without me but in this instance, I found out I'm not forgotten.

The day started in the sanctuary at Atlanta Unity Church, where I was the associate minister. The space seated four to five hundred people, and had seven steps leading to the platform where services were conducted, including weddings. A two-story wall of glass showcased the gigantic trees and lush greenery of the property. Outside, at the peak of the roof hung a string of silver flags like the ones in used car lots to get your attention. They fluttered in the wind and were meant to keep woodpeckers away from the wood exterior which didn't work but no one ever bothered to take the flags down.

The groom's parents had come from Serbia to attend their only son's wedding and since this was during the war between Kosovo and Serbia, it was quite a feat that they were able to get out of the country. But they did, and the smiles my groom's folks had on their faces were priceless.

The couple were nervous, as brides and grooms often are, but you and I know how love eventually overrules anything in its way because its call of Love is so strong. The ceremony went off well, without any problems. The thank you's I received afterward were a welcome relief.

Since I'd recently graduated from seminary, leading marriage rituals was foreign to me, and I wasn't comfortable with the role or all that familiar with my wedding text yet.

People were congratulating the couple and their wedding party in the narthex so I gathered my brown wedding binder, my purse and the high heels I exchanged for comfortable loafers. I expected to slip out unnoticed.

In the big meeting room where the reception was going to take place, staff were starting to set up the tables and chairs. I headed through the room to the parking lot. On the left was the door to a large storage room where everything unused was out of sight. The groom's father, with his round, rosy cheeks, opened the door and motioned in broken English to come into the room. "Aren't you staying for the festivities?" he asked.

"Thank you, but I have two dogs at home I need to feed," I answered. Ergo, this was an excuse I was trying out to contend with anyone insisting I stay longer. FYI, I'm a homebody so that's another reason I don't stay for receptions.

"Well, then, would you come in here, please? I have something I want to give you."

He waved me toward the door. Inside the room, I saw about a dozen oval serving trays balanced between chair seats like a bridge. Each serving tray held dozens of crystal aperitif glasses which he was filling with the squat bottle in his hands. He picked up one of the full delicate glasses that had a sand-blasted rose on it and handed it to me. I can feel how light that crystal was as if I still had it in my hand. "This is wine I made on the day my son was born," he told me. "I made it to serve on his wedding day."

I could imagine the joy and certainty he must have felt as he made the wine some twenty-five years earlier. His actions felt full of love and hope for the future of their newborn baby.

The planning and effort that went into making this wine, storing it for over a quarter of a century years AND getting it into the United States during a time of war in his country were astonishing.

Since then I have discovered the tradition of making wine on a son or daughter's birth day is not uncommon in Eastern Europe. If only our own culture had more meaningful traditions to pass on from generation to generation. More than overeating on holidays or setting off disruptive fireworks that scare the daylights out of our pets, this wine-making tradition took years to complete. We can barely sit still while our computers take longer than thirty seconds to boot up!

I share this story with my couples now and then because if it inspires them to think about what they can do to start and pass on a tradition in their family, all the better. For example, the box from their Anniversary Box ceremony can be passed on with a bottle of wine purchased on the day or week of the birth of a child. Or their Fisherman's Knot or Hand Fasting cords can be passed on and added on to by the new couple. A larger than normal central Sand Ceremony vessel can have sand from new beaches by the next generation getting married.

These are the kinds of things that add dazzle and meaning to already special occasions with the benefit of the stories told around that tradition.

I can still taste that wine in my mouth. It was very, very delicious, like a sweet liquid berry that warmed my heart. I was honored to share that wine for all its hope for the future.

Photo by Cottonbro, pexels.com

55 WINE BLENDING

In general, the wine blending is done with a white and red wine.

Combining the two different types of wine is symbolic of bringing two different lives together and making something totally new and unique. What people don't always remember is we blend not only our good qualities but also the character traits that are our greatest challenge to wholeness.

In the Bit of Dazzle below, you'll find a suggestion of wines the officiant can suggest to her/his couple. Blending white and red wine doesn't always taste good, which is an opportunity to remind them marriage is "for better or worse."

Supplies
Wine Carafes with the two chosen wines, water or juices*
Empty Carafe
Common Cup (a nice-sized wine glass)
Music to play while couple blends the wines together

Script
Officiant: [Couple's Names] are going to perform a Unity Wine Blending Ceremony as a symbol of their marriage. One carafe contains red wine representing the deep richness of the love in their hearts and the robust energy which keeps their loving relationship going.

The other carafe contains white wine, and it represents the strength of a loving marriage and a lingering taste in their soul for the love they feel for each other.

They will combine some of the two wines into the Common Cup, creating a rosé, which is symbolic of a committed relationship that blends ideas, negotiates habits and reveals the benefits of compromise in marriage. Some of the wine will remain in their individual carafes which represents that despite their blending, each of them remain unique and separate individuals.

[Couple's Names] please pour some of the wine from your carafe into the Common Cup.

Music may play.

Officiant *picks up the Common Cup.*

This cup is a sign of your unity. You are two distinct persons, respecting each other as equals, and you have chosen to join your today and tomorrows together, to build a life and seek your happiness together. When you drink from the same cup, with its sweetness and its bitterness, may it be a loving reminder that you will share pain and pleasure, struggle and hope.

Officiant *offers the Common Cup to the couple.*

Now is the time to further symbolize the unity of your minds, hearts and bodies. May this cup give you the taste for a life of adventure, growth, peace and happiness. May your lives be sweet and full to overflowing.

[Partner1] takes the Common Cup, sips and toasts [Partner2]. Hands the cup to his/her partner. [Partner2] takes the Common Cup, sips and toasts [Partner1]. Places the Common Cup back on the table and returns to their place with the officiant.

Officiant: This ceremony represents your two individual lives, combined like the two wines into one single life. The drinking of the combined wine signifies the commitment you now make to live your lives as one family. May you remember this day of commitment you have sealed with drinking of the new wine joining your lives as one.

A Bit of Dazzle

An alternative to swirling white and red wine together is to use one or the other -- a white or red wine and blend with a fruit juice or water. In planning with the couple, the officiant can discuss whether the meaning of the blending will be changed. Even though the tasting can be much more pleasant, like in the Bread and Salt ceremony, people can benefit from being aware of the fact that there are good times AND bad times, challenging times, and times of celebration. If this is an option the couple likes, the following is a suggested script.

Optional Script

Officiant: However, there are times when the blending of two different wines can be bitter, and just as importantly, a couple can weather the storms that are natural in all relationships. There may be good times and bad times; there may be a better and a worse.

56 WINE, ANNIVERSARY, LOVE LETTERS BOX

Background

Back in the Roman empire, wine was linked to rank and status, and a wine drinker was judged on a number of things from the origin of the wine, vintage, grape variety, and, importantly, an individual's capacity to hold one's drink. The quality of wine was also important in 5th century Greece, where wine was sealed in jars before it was shipped out to ensure it was truly the real deal.

Another fun fact is in "ye old" Europe, women were often the bartenders, so wine became associated with fertility and growth.

In earlier times, a good harvest was essential in order to ensure the survival of a community, wine came to represent fertility and it was used to bless the land. The drink was also linked to fertility due to its ability to lower inhibitions and therefore, by extension, boost the population; it gave longevity to existing communities and encouraged the production of new generations.

A Consideration

The Christian use of wine is around communion – infusing the receiver with the power and blessing of Jesus Christ. Because Jesus turned water to wine as his first miracle, wine carries for some people, very distinct religious meanings. Hence, you have to make sure the meaning of the wine is clear.

This is an extremely romantic and practical ceremony. A bottle of wine, and letters from each partner to one another are sealed into a box with nails.

If ever the marriage is in serious crisis the couple can open the box, read each other's letters, and share the wine together to remind them of what led them to their commitment and provide some thoughtful perspective on whatever the problem might be.

A couple can opt to include letters from their bridal party, too. Hopefully they'll never need to open it, but it addresses the fact that marriages aren't always smooth sailing, but creating this emergency kit can help a couple stay prepared if or when they ever experience challenges.

No Wine Option

If a couple doesn't drink alcohol, they can also write love letters to each other which they place in the box and latch, without any wine. Year after year they place a letter to each other in the box, read each letter the next year, evaluate their progress and set new goals. They can also create one letter together naming shared goals for their relationship. When they latch the box, they should make a statement together, such as "So it is," "Amen," or "Here we go." Encourage them to have fun with this process. (See Script below).

Supplies

Wine

Wine box with lock or latch – See Link Directory for featured box by Autumn Woodwork on Etsy

Love letters

Table for wine box

Decision by the couple—Open the box in an emergency, or in one year or five years

Instructions

Prior to their wedding day, request the couple put their love letters in envelopes that will fit into the box easily.

Directions for couples writing love letters

Take time apart to consider your current feelings about your partner. Only undertake this process when you feel a lot of love and respect for one another. It's better to put the process off until positive vibes are being exchanged, more so than doing it just because it's your anniversary. You can do this together or separately--your choice.

Couple Letter Writing Process

Take a few deep breaths and take your attention of your wedding to do list. Take a minute to enjoy being focused on the love you feel and being centered in the feelings you have for your partner. Set the intention that you are about to put into words your hopes and dreams for your partner and for your relationship together.

- Name 1-3 qualities you deeply love and appreciate about your partner
- Name something you 've already accomplished together
- Set out 3-5 intentions for the coming year
- Even though the box will be opened on your anniversary the following year, end your letter with "It is our intention to see these goals, dreams, and wishes become reality in one year, on (your anniversary date)."
- Sign and have fun with your signature such as using your pet names or make up a name that points toward your goals together. Examples: Your Dancing Deva Wife, Cindy, Happy CEO Husband, Kevin.

Script

Officiant: A bottle of wine has been placed in this box. (May tell a story or give details about meaning of wine chosen.) Wine represents the power of transformation, from a grape hanging on a vine into a delicious liquid. The intention here today is to set into motion that same transformational energy so it will flow continually into your relationship together, bringing renewal and all the ways two people delight in each other.

[Couple's Names] have written love letters to each other. [Couple's Names], you may now place the love letters you have written into the box.

Couple puts letters into the box.

Officiant: This is the time for you to seal the box, (with nails or close the latch) signifying your commitment to rely on each other in all ways and that your love and consideration of each other is firmly sealed.

Box is closed.

Officiant: In ___ years, (Couple chooses one- or five-year time delay) on (date), you'll open the box, and read the letters. You'll share the wine to remind you of what led you to your commitment and celebrate your growth and joy during the last (time frame). This will also be a time to provide some thoughtful perspective on any problems you may be facing together.

This Wine/Anniversary Box can help you remember what drew you together on this day, and renew your commitment to continue to imagine and create anew what the next (time period) years may bring.

Couple steps back to their starting position with officiant.

No Wine/Love Letters Option Script

Officiant: [Couple's Names] have written love letters to each other. They are a team, and the importance of the letters they'll be placing in this box are meant to bring them together to remember and also to plan for the next steps into their future. By setting aside time, they can be sure they'll be tending to their happiness and success as a couple.

[Couple's Names], you may now place in this box the love letters you have written into the box.

Couple puts their letters into the box.

Officiant: This is the time for you to seal the box, signifying your commitment to rely on each other in all ways and that your love and consideration of each other is firmly sealed.

Box is closed and latched.

Officiant: Next year, on (Anniversary date), open the box, and read the letters. You'll hopefully laugh and remember important moments you shared on your wedding day. But most importantly, celebrate your growth and joy during the last year. After you've read each other's letter, this can be a time to provide some thoughtful perspective on any problems you may be facing together.

This Love Letters Box can help you remember what drew you together on this day, and renew your commitment to continue to imagine and create anew what the next (time period) years may bring.

Then write two more love letters and put them all into the box to be read the following year. Make this a tradition in your family!

Optional: If letters have been included from the parents or attendants, officiant says: "Know that when you open the box on your anniversary, all of our love and faith in you and the love you've found will be waiting for you to enjoy."

A Bit of Dazzle

*Find a couple of wines that will blend well together—like Champagne and burgundy (which makes Cold Duck). Mix Chardonnay with Grenache to create a rosé.

If the couple has written personal vows to each other that they share privately, these vows can be put into this box instead of a letter.

Letters of support and encouragement can be written by the couple's wedding party, parents and/or siblings.

You may want to collect these letters at the rehearsal from the wedding party and bundle them together this way: all of the bridesmaids' letters are bundled and the maid/matron of honor places them in the box during the ceremony, and likewise the groomsmen's letters are bundled and placed in the box by the Best Man.

If parents write letters you can include them in placing them in the box as part of the experience.

Another dazzle is whether you place these letters into the box during the ceremony, or they're already in the box and you tell the guests that these other special letters are in the Wine Box, it is your choice.

NOTE: Make sure the box is big enough to handle the letters and the wine.

If there's a friend or family member who is a woodworker, they can be enlisted to make the special box for the wine. Then you can add to the ceremony at the start, "The beautiful box on this altar table was made by _____. (Describe box and ay important details if applicable).

ADDENDUM

Curating Questionnaire

One way to use this book is to let it be a set of four or five scripts an officiant can use to curate special ceremonies and offer them to your couple. These suggested questions will help to understand what your couple might be interested in.

1. What cultural tradition would you like to incorporate, adapt or investigate as a possibility for your ceremony?

2. What special rituals have you seen at wedding ceremonies or in videos that you're curious about including in your experience?

3. Chose one

☐   We are traditional

☐   We are open to trying something new

☐   Let's create something original

4. Would you like your ceremony to be interactive – others have a role to play?

5. What kinds of physical elements do you like? Underline all that apply.
Stones, Sand, Water, Fire, Glass, Wine, Pottery, Mead/Beer, Sound, Herbs, Trees, Flowers

6. Do you want to have a memento left over from your special ceremony that you can display or pass on to your children?

☐ Yes   ☐ No   ☐ No preference

7. Choose one time frame you'd like your entire ceremony to last.

☐ 10 minutes   ☐ 15 minutes   ☐ 20 minutes
☐ 25 -30 minutes   ☐ Longer than 30 minutes

8. Please tell me anything you'd like me to consider in curating the best selections for you to choose from.

21 Ways to Ask Guests to Turn Their Cell Phones Off

Even when a couple has a sign that reminds people to turn their cell phones off, and though most people are aware they should turn them off, it's often preferred that the officiant or DJ reminds people to turn their phones off before the ceremony begins. Here's some elaborate, some easy and even fun ways to ask folks to give their technology a rest.

1. Call the groomsmen at the same time and they all answer their cell phones together. During the faked chaos, the officiant can say, "See how important it is to get your phones turned off?"

2. Have the Bridesmaids take out their phones and call the Groomsmen and remind them to turn their phones off. Then announce the couple requests an unplugged ceremony.

3. If the DJ has sound effects, play a ring tone and the attendants whip their phones out just as all are set in their positions.

4. Ask everyone to pull out their phone, take a selfie and send it to Partner1 or Partner2 so they can see a different side of the preparations, then turn their phone off.

5. We wish to remind you to please turn off your cell phone ringer and refrain from using your cell phone during the wedding ceremony. Thank you!

6. The couple really wants to see your faces, not your devices. Please put away your camera and phone until after the ceremony.

7. [Couple's Names] want to be present with you on their special day. That's why the request that you please keep your phones and cameras turned off during the ceremony. They will happily share the photos that are captured today by their photographer.

8. For real, put your phones away please so [Couple's Names] can share their love with you, all hands open and free today.

9. Welcome family and friends! [Couple's Names] have hired a photographer to capture how this moment looks with their camera, so you can capture how it feels with your hearts.

10. There's a pro here taking pictures – [Couple's Names] asked them to come. Please rest your cameras as their ceremony only needs one!

11. As our couple tie the knot, please be their guest. Their photographer will take care of the rest!

12. The greatest gift you can give [Couple's Names] today is to be truly present, so please turn off all phones and cameras and enjoy this special moment with them.

13. Please switch off your devices and stow them away, [Couple's Names] would love to see your smiles aiming their way.

14. Thank you for coming! [Couple's Names] have but one plea for you. Please keep their ceremony camera-free. Though their I Do's are unplugged, [Couple's Names] reception is not. Once their vows are exchanged, you're free to take a shot!

15. Please honor [Couple's Names] wishes with no photos until I pronounce them Mr. and Mrs.!

16. [Couple's Names] want you to be able to relax and have fun with them today! This in mind, I've been asked by [Couple's Names] to invite you to put down all your favorite devices and just be present in the moment with them. Please leave your camera in your bag because our couple has made sure great photography is covered! Put your cell phone on mute I promise they'll call back!

17. [Couple's Names] are happy to share their professional wedding photos later, but the greatest gift you can give them today is just being fully here in this sacred and special moment.

18. The bride and groom have asked that you share in their wedding fully and not through the lens of a camera or cell phone.

19. The bride and groom have asked me to respectfully suggest guests put down their electronics and just enjoy the day. For [Couple's Names] sake, would you please put your camera or phone away?

20. Ladies and gentlemen, prior to wedding take-off, all seat backs and tray tables must be in their upright and locked positions, all bags properly stowed, and all portable electronic devices turned off and stowed. This includes cell phones and cameras.

21. As Shakespeare once said, "Please turn off your cell phones."

LINK DIRECTORY

This directory is for those who have purchased the printed copy of Anthology of Special Ceremonies. *These links are embedded in the text of the corresponding ceremony in the eBook.*

Native American Blanket Ceremony

Color Meanings Symbolism of North American Native Indians https://www.warpaths2peacepipes.com/native-american-symbols/color-meanings-symbolism.htm- :~:text=Red%3A Faith, Beauty and Happiness,Blue%3A Wisdom and Intuition%3A Confidence.

Bourbon Unity Ceremony #1

Complete guide to whiskey blending wedding ceremonies https://whiskeymade.com/whiskey-wedding-guide/how-to-have-a-whiskey-blending-wedding-ceremony/

Whiskey Wedding Resource for barrels, whiskey, and bottles https://whiskeymade.com/whiskey-wedding-guide

Bread and Salt

YouTube Bread and Salt Blessing video: https://www.youtube.com/watch?v=QBdpMCI56vg

Korovai bread recipe: https://lyukum.com/korovai-1-0/

Andre Aciman Quotes: https://www.brainyquote.com/authors/andre-aciman-quotes

Breaking of the Glass video

Excellent YouTube exploration of the tradition--Why Break a Glass at Weddings?

Professor Shalom Sabar, https://youtu.be/Gpbhtq10qlY

Christian Cross

Enacted on Pinterest: https://www.pinterest.com/pin/526287906453026203/

Coin and Lasso Ceremony

Find a Lasso

https://www.etsy.com/search?q=laso%20for%20wedding&ref=auto1&as_prefix=laso

https://www.weddingarras.com/wedding-lazos-wedding-lassos.htm#silver

Wedding Coins

https://www.etsy.com/search?q=wedding%20coins

https://www.weddingarras.com/wedding-coins-and-wedding-arrascoins.htm

Coins, boxes, lassos:

https://www.etsy.com/shop/JMcKinleyCorp?ref=simple-shop-header-name&listing_id=294034521

Romans 12: https://www.blueletterbible.org/kjv/rom/12/1/s_1058001

Arras and Lasso ceremony on YouTube:
https://www.youtube.com/watch?v=gs7GQheTz5g

Divorce Ceremony

US Census Bureau Divorce Statistics, 2020
https://www.census.gov/library/stories/2020/12/united-states-marriage-and-divorce-rates-declined-last-10-years.html
It's over Easy – 48 Divorce Statistics in 2020
https://www.itsovereasy.com/insights/divorce-statistics

Ken and Judy Grimes
http://www.northernmichiganministers.com/

Grayson Perry: Rites of Passage, video
https://www.youtube.com/watch?v=QbeW-Yw2pR0

Transformative Rituals: Celebrations for Personal Growth by Gay and
David Williamson. Available on Amazon.com--
https://www.amazon.com/Transformative-Rituals-Celebrations-Personal-Growth/dp/155874293X

Flower Ceremony

Research what different colors of roses mean:
https://www.floraly.com.au/blogs/news/rose-symbolism-colours-and-meanings

For flowers other than roses, and their symbolic meaning:
https://fieldofflowers.com/about-us/flower-meanings/

Glass Bead Ceremony

Glass beads available on Etsy

Unity Ceremony Keepsake Blown Glass Piece

https://www.etsy.com/listing/610980440/unity-ceremony-keepsake-blown-glass?ga_order=most_relevant&ga_search_type=all&ga_view_type=gallery&ga_search_query=glass+bowl+piece&ref=sr_gallery-1-1&organic_search_click=1&frs=1

Handfasting Ceremony

Handfasting cords

https://www.etsy.com/search?q=handfasting%20cord&ref=auto1&as_prefix=handfasting

Download of three Handfasting scripts: https://northern-michiganweddingofficiants.com/wp-content/uploads/2019/02/Handfasting-Handout.pdf

Hawaii Wedding Traditions

Hawaiian Wedding Song sung by Elvis Presley in 1961:
https://youtu.be/R1GPK4Mx_lg

Somewhere Over the Rainbow sung by Israel "IZ" Kamakawiwoʻole recorded in 2010: https://youtu.be/V1bFr2SWP1I

Shaka Leis: https://shakalei.com/wedding-leis/

Jumping the Broom

https://www.pinterest.com/pin/365424957264775630/

Custom Wedding Broom
www.etsy.com/listing214976499/custom-wedding-broom-jumping-broom

Patricia Burgess, Your Wedding, Your Way: https://your-wedding-your-way-wedding-service.business.site/

Ketubah

Examples of Ketubah Directory
https://www.etsy.com/search?q=ketubah%20modern&ref=auto-1

Nehama Samson, Ketubah artist
https://www.etsy.com/listing/621130810/modern-ketubah-arttree-heart-beach-2?ga_order=most_relevant&ga_search_type=all&ga_view_type=gallery&ga_search_query=ketubah+modern&ref=sr_gallery-1-43&organic_search_click=1&frs=1&sca=1

Love Locks Ceremony

YouTube ceremony in action: https://youtu.be/zrlobfv_-dg

Love Locks, Ivan Kostyrya, WoodbaobabUA,
https://www.etsy.com/listing/1182284799/family-values-personalized-gift
Kherson, Ukraine. Please support his site.

Supplies on Etsy
https://www.etsy.com/market/love_lock_ceremony

Mead Ceremony

Mead recipe from Grow, Forage, Cook, Ferment
https://www.growforagecookferment.com/hot-to-make-a-gallong-of-mead/

Photos of Marriage Cups
https://www.google.com/search?output=search&tbm=isch&q=What+is+a+marriage+cup?&source=iu&ictx=1&fir=_0FRFUXOiYVjHM%252CL40-74l8sj0rIM%252C_&vet=1&usg=AI4_-kSzbCVBhrMLiCF5twGrxsZZHhudWQ&sa=X&ved=2ahUKEwiVu_mZ2vTyAhVMGVkFHeqVAREQ9QF6BAgNEAE#imgrc=_0FRFUXOiYVjHM

Featured Loving Cup: https://PagePottery.com

Puzzle Ceremony

Variety of wedding puzzles on Etsy
https://www.etsy.com/listing/886166285/family-values-personalized-gift-wedding

Ivan Kostryrya: https://www.etsy.com/shop/WoodbaobabUA?ref=l2-about-shopname

Wedding Zen

Christopher Shelley on Facebook
https://www.facebook.com/christopher.shelley.5621
Website: http://www.illuminatingceremonies.com

Affiliate link for the book, Best. Ceremony. Ever.
https://amzn.to/3uTVOWE

Sand Ceremony, #9

Available on Etsy
https://www.etsy.com/market/unity_sand_frame

Available on Amazon
https://www.amazon.com/unity-sand-frame/s?k=unity+sand+frame

Rite of the Seven Steps

Bit of Dazzle Stake supplier
https://www.google.com/search?q=wedding+jar+stakes&sxsrf=AOaemvIX7p_t8g1-Ysas-Klp88K7Swv7SA:1631827797068&tbm=isch&source=iu&ictx=1&fir=uPO5LZmoiaQQ0M%252CvJsBLaKpKtw0wM%252C_&vet=1&usg=AI4_-kS5WmH-1oUnpKxJzAzLHcHV7GZA2w&sa=X&ved=2ahUKEwijt7ahuITzAhXQZc0KHea9DhUQ9QF6BAgKEAE#imgrc=uPO5LZmoiaQQ0M

Wikipedia on the 7 Steps
https://en.wikipedia.org/wiki/Symbolism_of_the_number_7

Stefana Crowns

10% discount on Stefana crowns
https://www.etsy.com/shop/contemporaryvision?coupon=CONTEMPORARY10

Traditional version of Greek Stefana ceremony
https://www.crownstefana.com/greek-orthodox-weddings/

Greek Orthodox ceremony on YouTube
https://youtu.be/DgrjvBl3ut4

Big Fat Greek Wedding trailer
https://www.youtube.com/watch?v=O2mecmDFE-Q

Stringing the Pearls

Video: https://northern-michiganweddingofficiants.com/pearls/
Or
YouTube: https://www.youtube.com/watch?v=t0aDm0Pe1FM&t=55s

Tree Planting

OneTreePlanted.org
https://onetreeplanted.org/ or search for "non-profit tree planters"

Truce Bells

Bells
https://Bellsonline.net

Small Bells for Guests
https://www.bellsonline.net/smallbells.aspx

FactoryDirectCraft.com
https://factorydirectcraft.com/catalog/categories/1302_2533_680-bells.html

Bells on Amazon.com
https://www.amazon.com/Maydahui-Vintage-Training-Housebreaking-christmas/dp/B07F151GMK/ref=sr_1_29_sspa?dchild=1&gclid=CjwKC
Ajw7rWKBhAtEiwAJ3CWLNf83lItzSY0jGplIUcJTyqNbBFo0JkrFTwbU
YhuK6azelo73SVx0BoCVFwQAvD_BwE&hvadid=177576880756&hvdev
=c&hvlocphy

Photo by permission pexels-arthousestudios.com

Unity Reaction Ceremony

Photo of special wedding ceremony using Unity Reaction:
https://thefirstyearblog.com/wp-content/uploads/2013/04/Rustic-Wedding-Unity-Reaction.jpg

Disappearing ink – because this is such a long link, search Amazon for "disappearing ink"

Precautions for handling Sodium Hydroxide
https://www.chemicalsafetyfacts.org/sodium-hydroxide/

Purchase Sodium Hydroxide
http://www.dudadiesel.com/choose_item.php?id=2drhdl

Valentines Day Background

Wikipedia accounting of the origins of Valentines
https://en.wikipedia.org/wiki/Valentine%27s_Day

Native American Wedding Vases

https://www.kachinahouse.com/native-american-pottery/wedding-vases

Wedding Zen

Best. Ceremony. Ever. (Affiliate link)
https://www.amazon.com/gp/product/1682682854/ref=as_li_tl?ie=UTF8&camp=1789&creative=9325&creativeASIN=1682682854&linkCode=as2&tag=io2021-20&linkId=1025b14c36dc4a0e3b000c3f0c4e7142

Chris' website: http://www.illuminatingceremonies.com/

Wine, Anniversary or Love Letters Box

www.etsy.com/listing/784113957/wine-box-separate-space-for-a-usb-and

ACKNOWLEDGEMENTS

In the movie, Field of Dreams, Kevin Costner (my heartthrob) tells Terrence Mann, "There comes a time when all the cosmic tumblers have clicked into place and the Universe opens itself up and shows you for a few seconds what's possible." Being from the '60's myself, I never expected the Universe to open me up to ministry when I was a Janis Joplin loving hippie. I've been lucky to have found friends and supporters who have appreciated, aided, and abetted my irreverence as well as my seriousness. I was ordained by the Unity School of Practical Christianity in 1990. I love the spiritual roots it gave me and the freedom to come from my heart, and not dogma.

Ceremony was my strong point in ministerial school, and Judy Grimes was the course instructor where I learned how to lead a wedding ceremony. She encouraged me to be creative and experiment.

Little did I know that some 20 years later, Judy would pave the way for me lead the local Unity Church and get incorporated into the area where weddings take place in nearly every nook, cranny, beach, and vineyard.

Judy married Ken Grimes, a Lutheran minister and author. Ken became my grammatical, comma-correcting proofreader, and editor. Thank you, Ken, for your generosity of spirit and talent. I'm glad you loved the rum cake.

Since I was ordained in 1990, I tried my hand leading churches, and part of the work was doing weddings. Which is where an important tumbler fell into place by meeting Chris Hume. She's helped me see what's possible since we first met in Atlanta. She is wise and wonderful, and my best friend. Her support led to creating this Treasury.

I continued to experiment with the power of ritual by changing how a wedding proceeds from one element to another, and amending the content from traditional to imaginative. My couples brought to me some of the best ideas and resources. Thanks to all 1400 of them because they are in this book as well.

Even though the Wedding Ceremony Podcast isn't live anymore, Clint Hufft and JP Reynolds gave me so many ideas through their conversations. Some of those ideas are now ceremonies in this Treasury, so thank you two for inspiring me and so many other officiants, all over the globe.

One of the people who patiently waited for me to find the right avenue for my expertise was my local BFF, Donna LaVoie. Because I've had a bad habit of worrying, when I told her I was putting this book together, she was 100 times more enthusiastic about it than she ever was about any of the courses I created and helped keep me going. Her ability to spot inconsistencies and point out better wording has been very helpful.

Becky Brough-Oberrecht, one of my BFF's from high school, along with her hubby Keith, proofread and edited in their spare time from Alaska. I'm so grateful to have such a long-time friend be one of the reoccurring tumblers clicking into place in my life.

Thank you, everyone.

ABOUT THE AUTHOR

Crystal Yarlott led her first wedding ceremony the same year she was ordained by Unity School in 1990. She left church ministry in 2010, and became a full-time officiant. She's conducted wedding ceremonies for over 1400 people in Georgia, North Carolina and Michigan. She lives in the tip of the mitt of Michigan where weddings happen in vineyards, on beaches, in barns, tops of mountains, national parks, private homes, yachts and tall ships, and last but not least, ski slopes. She lives with her three dogs and two cats just outside of Traverse City. Her website is NMIWO.com